# Futuring Your Church

# futuring your church

## finding. . . your vision and making it work

George B. Thompson Jr.

United Church Press
Cleveland, Ohio

United Church Press, Cleveland, Ohio 44115
© 1999 by George B. Thompson Jr.

Excerpts from *Church Leadership: Vision, Team, Culture,
and Integrity* by Lovett H. Weems Jr. (Nashville: Abingdon
Press, 1993). Used by permission of Abingdon Press. • Excerpts
from Mission and Vision Statements of First Community
Church reprinted by permission. • Excerpts from Mission
and Vision Statement of Resurrection MCC reprinted
by permission.

Biblical quotations are from the New Revised Standard Version of the Bible,
© 1989 by the Division of Christian Education of the National Council of the
Churches of Christ in the U.S.A., and are used by permission.
Adaptations have been made for inclusivity.

Published 1999. All rights reserved

Printed in the United States of America on acid-free paper

04   03   02   01   00   99      5   4   3   2   1

Library of Congress Cataloging-in-Publication Data

Thompson, George B. (George Button), 1951–
    Futuring your church : finding your vision and making it work /
George B. Thompson, Jr.
        p.   cm.
    Includes bibliographical references.
    ISBN 0-8298-1331-4 (pbk. : alk. paper)
    1. Church growth.   I. Title.
BV652.25.T48   1999
254'.5—dc21                                                98-50329
                                                              CIP

*To Ann Page-El,*
*Christian educator and friend,*
*One who lifts the spirit with encouragement*

# CONTENTS

# PREFACE

M Y GRANDMOTHER GREW UP in a mud-and-sod lean-to in eastern Montana. The home had no running water or electricity. Neighbors got around on foot, on horseback, and, on special occasions, by horse-drawn buggy. Her life and theirs were pretty simple and close to a land that was not always friendly.

By the time that my grandmother died at the ripe old age of ninety-two, the world had become a vastly different place. It was not just the dramatic development of the radio or the horseless carriage of my grandmother's youth. Grandma also saw air flight, jet planes, atomic bombs, satellites, space walks, television, and microcomputers burst onto the scene. Her life was prolonged by two surgeries, for conditions that would have killed her in her youth. Yet my grandmother, despite all these amazing changes, chose to keep to a simple and familiar life. And it served her just fine.

It would be nice if we could say the same for today's churches, but we cannot. Grandma could choose to overlook many new things about the world and still maintain for herself a worthwhile, satisfactory life. Yet if groups of people do the same, their joint efforts eventually will fade and die. Today's churches are watching new things appear on the horizon virtually every year. What happens if they ignore the new things? Can congregations that try to live only by the past have much of a future?

This book was born out of the conviction that the world of the twenty-first century will not allow vibrant, effective churches to stand still. When things around us change, we in the churches need to assess where we are and where we could be going. But how? Do we know what to do that will help us obtain a full and clear picture of ourselves, our situations, and our possibilities?

A second conviction leading to the writing of this book is that being prepared for the future takes more than good fortune or more of the same. Congregations that seek to follow God's leading into the future need to understand what they are facing, what to listen to, and how to put themselves into a position to hear the Holy Spirit speak new things. What follows is my attempt to show leaders of such congregations how to go about such a complex, yet rewarding and blessed, enterprise.

In preparing this book, I have been shaped by my particular background and experiences. For two decades, I have served on the pastoral staffs of Protestant congregations in several traditions and in several regions of the United States. These experiences were quite diverse in many ways. Yet I began to be aware of some patterns that these churches seemed to share in spite of their differences. These common patterns, and the reasons for their appearance, became a subject of my study, reflection, and testing. What is presented here has been honed with a number of congregations, pastoral workshops, seminary courses, and training projects.

The First Plymouth Foundation, Englewood, Colorado, provided major funding for congregational training with early versions of this material. I thank the pastors and lay leaders of the following Colorado United Church of Christ congregations: First, Arvada; Christ Congregational, Denver; Kirk of Bonnie Brae, Denver; Christ Congregational, Ft. Morgan; and Faith, Windsor. I also thank First Congregational, Boulder, for financial assistance; the Rev. Bill Dalke, Rocky Mountain Conference Minister, for his collegial support; and Virginia DeRolf for invaluable advice and encouragement. In Michigan, the Comstock Fund of First Congregational UCC Church, Alpena, provided major funding. Pastor Bob Case has offered gracious guidance. Thanks go to the pastors and leaders of the following Michigan United Church of Christ churches: Congregational, Breckenridge; Peace, Detroit; First Congregational, Morenci; and Zion, Mt. Clemens.

This book is dedicated to Ann Page-El, Christian educator and friend. Her faith and ministry—not to mention her encouragement—continue to inspire my vocational efforts.

# Calling

## Being Intentional about Your Church's Future

**1**

WHAT IS YOUR CONGREGATION LIKE? How would you describe it to someone who has never participated in any of its activities? Which aspects of its life would you mention first: its building, worship services, people, theological beliefs, music, youth ministry, mission giving, educational programs, hands-on community service, the pastor? With what would you want this prospective visitor to be impressed? Later, if you asked this person whether your congregation was looking forward or backward, what would she or he say?

### Does God Call Congregations Today?

One of the Bible's major themes is that of being called. Yahweh called Noah to construct a vessel in which to preserve all kinds of living creatures from the great Flood. Yahweh called Sarai and Abram late in midlife to leave their comfortable urban home and travel to an as-yet-unknown new land. That journey lasted for generations and includes the call of Moses. Saved from certain death as a baby and raised in Pharaoh's household, Moses unexpectedly and reluctantly led the Israelites out of slavery in Egypt and farther toward their land of promise. Yahweh called Samuel as a young boy to serve his people as both a priest and a prophet; Samuel eventually anointed Israel's first two kings. Yahweh called Isaiah, when he was worshiping in the Temple, to tell his own people that ruin was on its way unless they repented. Jesus called twelve men to a special role in his ministry. Paul was called to take the good news beyond the confines of Judea and Judaism.

Does God still call congregations today? Paul's letters to young churches in the Greco-Roman world certainly suggest so. Something about the Christian witness of the people as a community seems to have lived at the heart of Paul's messages to the scattered believers. He told them to avoid divisions and unite in their thinking (1 Cor. 1:10). In Romans and Galatians, he reminded them that they stood for particular beliefs, such as grace and freedom from legalistic religion. Most of Paul's extant letters were written to congregations rather than to individuals. Even Philemon, which sounds like a personal note, used the "eavesdropping" congregation as pressure to persuade an influential church member to do what Paul wanted.

Indeed, God calls congregations. So a call, like a journey, means that those who are being called are looking ahead of, not just behind, themselves. That imaginary description that you gave to a prospective visitor: Did it reveal a congregation that is looking ahead? Is your congregation aware of its call now into the future?

## Why Bother with the Future?

Some church people object to focusing on the future. They might claim that no one knows what the future holds. Others might note wryly that we will all get to the future one way or another. Still others could point to the congregation's long survival without worry. Can it not continue pretty much as it has before? Probably not.

Since the mid-1960s, something has been happening on the religious scene that should lead longtime church members to have serious concern. Standard-brand Protestant churches, so long the bastions of cultural civility, have been losing members. Not just a few here and there, but thousands upon thousands, year after year. Very likely you have some knowledge of this trend. But you may not realize how extensive it has been. Although peaking in 1964, membership in several Protestant traditions dropped steadily until, by 1991, its aggregate total was back to its level in 1949.[1] This amounts to a loss in the millions, or about 22 percent. For certain denominations, the loss figure is even higher.

Drastic numerical changes tell only a part of this story. The prominent role that this broad Protestant religious tradition has played in U.S. life also has shifted. Taken together, this "mainline" religion in the United States wielded the numbers, the inner drive, the influence in society, economics, and politics to mark the culture with its stamp. To be mainline Protestant was, in a significant way, to be truly American.[2] But this longstanding relationship has been changing before our eyes. By the 1980s, it had become clear to researchers in U.S. religion that this bulwark of religion and culture had split apart. The U.S. religious landscape is now more in flux; it is more complicated and much less defined by one flow of tradition. It is more identified by clusters of like mind than by official denominational structures.[3]

That is, the religion that dominated the United States when the baby boomers were babies is turning into a faded backdrop on the religious stage. It has lost its old, comfortable place. The way that things are going, this mainline Protestant tradition could erode easily into a fragile shell of its former self. Why? Explanations can be complex, but one factor has to be today's market-style social flavor. It seems that just about everything in U.S. life today can be bought and sold. The same appears to be true for religious participation. What used to be habitual for earlier generations of Americans now occurs much more by choice. Baby boomers do not go to church at the same rates as older Americans; neither do the "busters," the generation coming up behind the boomers. They live in an environment that encourages self-selection. This tendency makes life more complicated, especially when standard criteria for any such choices are not widely recognized.[4] If you do not "have to" go to church, and you do not think that you will get much out of it anyway, why bother?

So let us ask the earlier question again: Why should well-established churches today concern themselves with the way that the future is taking shape? Why should a young church do so, for that matter? The answer should be troubling to many of us: because the rules of the U.S. religious game have changed—whether we like it or not. Those of us who grew up in the former mainline traditions are not able to assume that what we do communicates anything of deep meaning, of spiritual faith, to anyone else.[5]

## What Is Needed to Look Forward?

Does your congregation look forward, or is it comfortable looking backward? If your congregation decided that it wanted to look forward, what would it need to take into account? Some scholars suggest that it would need to position itself creatively as a "community of memory," sharing its version of the Christian message in perhaps more limited ways.[6] Ironically, most people in the United States who do not go to church have more in common with basic mainline Protestantism than with a more conservative church style.[7] This insight suggests that there is great opportunity available if a church is willing to take on the challenge.

But what would such a challenge entail? Hadaway and Roozen see the need for intentional effort, acknowledging that the results will trigger changes—and some church members do not want changes, even if the changes would lead to more members.[8] That is, a church must be willing to take some risks if it is to have a strong future. Some pastors, as well as lay church leaders, shy away from such risk.[9] However, the prospect for the old mainline seems to be "no pain, no gain."

Even more effort is needed, Hadaway and Roozen claim, in congregations that are not growing numerically. For churches that have been stagnant, these researchers call for "lasting changes in the [congregation's] identity, vision and purpose."[10] Such changes, in terms of *content,* should concentrate upon helping new people be aware of God at work in the midst of worship.[11] Such changes, in terms of the congregation's structural *processes,* should concentrate upon being movementlike, that is, energetic and flexible rather than orderly and predictable.[12]

Hadaway and Roozen provide serious church leaders with a thoughtful and challenging outline for moving into the future. If you do not believe that they are telling the truth, then this book is not for you. For this book provides you with a map for futuring your church. This map centers on a process, a way of making the journey into the future. The way that we go about discovering our churches' futures will be critical to the discovery itself.

## The Book's Premises

The process that you will engage in this book, this "how" of discovery, has been built upon certain premises. One of these premises is that the large-scale forces that have led to the major changes described above can be understood and utilized. We may not like what we see going on around us, but we can learn to make sense of it. We even can be creative about how we learn to respond to it. Another premise is that whatever we do in our churches assumes some point of view. That is, decisions about the congregation's worship life, fellowship activities, education, facilities, operational processes, and so on flow out of perspectives that most members take for granted. We will solicit the help of several concepts throughout the book to help us be clearer about such perspectives as we discuss the futuring process.

The focus here is not on analysis, but on action. Nonetheless, I claim that doing what implicitly seems useful probably will not help your church. I have watched many congregations quietly worry about their future, then hire a pastor to "make things happen," as though being busy automatically will help the church. In this present era, futuring centers not on restructuring or program, but on vision (which we will discuss shortly). The action that the future calls forth from our churches today must be informed by new understandings, new frameworks.

This book primarily has in mind leaders of standard-brand Protestant congregations. However, because of the nature of this process, it should not be too difficult for industrious leaders from other Protestant traditions—not to mention Roman Catholic parishes and even Jewish synagogues—to make a few adaptations and find it effective for their situations. At the same time, though, this wide applicability of the process does *not* suggest that every religious congregation is prepared at every stage of its life to engage such a process beneficially. I can think of at least three scenarios that do not lend themselves to futuring: (1) there is an escalated conflict (i.e., one that has entered the public arena of the church); (2) the pastor and/or congregational leaders are not interested; and (3) the congregation is facing a crisis that is threatening closure.

In the first scenario, the conflict first must be worked through, and some form of reconciliation reached, before a futuring venture can be successfully undertaken. In the second scenario, the congregation must come to terms with the realities of its current leadership. A pastor or influential members who are content with the church's condition, or who are unwilling to lead into risk, cannot enlist the congregation to look clearly and honestly at where it is or where it could be headed. In the third scenario, the immediate crisis—usually about money or property—triggers such anxiety that the congregation is too paralyzed to look any further than the short term. Ironically, an effective or faithful solution to the immediate crisis would emerge best out of a new vision. The sad fact is that a congregation on the ropes usually is ill prepared to puts its energy to such wise use.

For the congregation that is strong enough and confident enough to seek God's leading, the journey to discover fresh, compelling vision will be challenging, exciting, and rewarding. Let us take a quick view of what that journey looks like, as it is developed in this book.

At the heart of every dynamic congregation is a strong vision. Vision is the central element to any adventure in futuring. In the last several years, business publications have devoted a significant amount of coverage to the notion of vision. This attention does not necessarily mean that lots of companies are transforming themselves with new vision, but it does mean that persons who study and assist businesses are becoming aware of the pivotal role that vision plays in any organization. Students and leaders of the church have not been ignorant of this trend. Lovett H. Weems Jr.'s book *Church Leadership* carries an entire chapter on the subject. There, Weems discusses vision in terms of several qualities; in my own words:[13]

1. Vision is not the same as mission (we will explore this distinction later)
2. There is something about it that is peculiar to your congregation
3. Its sights are set upon what is possible ahead, rather than upon what has occurred before
4. It reveals a desire to provide ministry beyond itself
5. It is grounded in current conditions
6. It also elevates the congregation's view of what is most important to it
7. It appeals and evokes interest and commitment
8. It is embraced by the congregation as a community
9. It speaks as both a challenging summons and a grace-filled opportunity
10. It generates optimism

According to Weems, vision will do these things for a congregation:[14]

- It draws the congregation together to pursue something together that is bigger than any individual member
- It invigorates and creates enthusiasm
- It is the basis for sorting out which issues are primary
- It becomes the overarching reference point for the congregation's life and ministry
- It points the congregation to a greater set of possibilities
- It becomes a magnet, luring others to its appeal

Vision is important to the congregation because, as Weems implies throughout these points, the healthy church coheres around it. When a church has a vision, when the vision is clear, inviting, and strong, the members know it. The community knows it. There is little ambiguity over what the congregation stands for and seeks to become. Weems's finely tuned summary of vision can assist your work throughout this book.

## A Vision Is Not a Mission Statement

Again, vision is not quite the same as mission. Mission statements have become a popular activity among businesses and not-for-profit organizations in the last several years. (A book has even been published that lists mission statements from three hundred companies.)[15] The distinction between vision and mission may seem at first to be a subtle one, yet that subtlety can make the difference.

Mission deals with concrete achievements; *vision* deals with the larger picture of aim, broad purpose, striving. The vision drives what becomes identified as the mission, not the other way around.[16] What tends to happen in churches is that a mission statement is developed, but it is so general in nature that it does not capture the special potential of the specific congregation.[17] Within themselves, mission statements do not generate the compelling images that can carry a community of faith into the future. That task is the realm of vision.

When one learns something of the history of an established congregation, one encounters bits and pieces of its earlier vision. That vision led an earlier generation of church members to follow it into the future with conviction and energy. Yet visions are not self-sustaining; they must be nurtured and nourished all along the way. One critique of U.S. Protestantism as it concludes the twentieth century is not that it is without vision, but that the vision has faded and become mostly unusable. As a feature of any particular congregation, vision can run along a continuum from "clear and strong" to "absent," with everything in between. Much has changed in our world since the end of World War II. The time for fresh vision has come.

## *A Vision Is a Constellation of Stars*

In the following process, I have chosen a metaphor that I hope conveys something of the quality and power of vision. This metaphor is the constellation and its stars. Think for a moment about what a constellation is. When we look up into a dark night sky, what do we see? Technically, of course, we see sparkles of light, most of which are emitted from stars. But for our purposes, we can say that what we see are the stars themselves—lots of them, in their awesome magnificence. Since ancient days, when our ancestors looked up into the sky, they also saw the stars making shapes and figures. They named these shapes and figures: the Big Dipper, the Northern Cross, the Pleiades, Cassiopeia, and so forth. We call these figures constellations—"stars with" one another. How are constellations created? Astronomy reminds us that the stars do not arrange themselves in the patterns. We humans do that.

A church's vision is like a constellation. It is a grouping of stars that create a shape and story in the perception of its beholders. When your congregation looks ahead into the future, what does it see? What image of a possible future does it behold? What are the stars making up that image? Why does the congregation see just those stars and not others?

For a congregation, stars for creating a compelling vision derive from three sources. Although it mixes metaphors a bit, I sometimes call these three sources the tripod for vitality, for all three must work together to get a good picture:

1. Heritage: all the elements of the congregation's past; its own particular history as well as that of the ecclesiastical tradition that gave it birth.
2. Context: everything that surrounds and permeates the congregation's environment, both the measurable features that we see in census reports and the sometimes elusive features of culture and local history.

3. Theological bearings: the way in which the congregation orients itself in light of its understanding of what God is like and how God acts; these bearings are both explicit and implicit, that is, they include our conscious expression of belief as well as our less-conscious, deep assumptions about the way the world is.

In chapters 2 through 4, we will examine each one of these legs of the tripod, these sources of stars. Processes and activities will be introduced so that the congregation's participation can be enlisted. These sets of activities will help you identify stars to be considered for your church's next constellation. Then, in chapter 5, you will bring the three sets of stars together. What do you hear them saying to one another? To your congregation? What constellation do you see beginning to emerge on the horizon of your congregation's future? You will ask these questions as you develop from the stars a working declaration of vision.

This declaration then will be the basis of chapter 6, the "So what?" chapter. So what difference does a fresh vision actually make in the life of the congregation? How should it affect the way that your church worships, how it teaches, nurtures, and cares for people, develops community, responds to human suffering, considers its use of resources, and in general shares the good news? Chapter 6 will show you a simple organization model that can guide you through the process (sometimes it will seem to be a maze) of applying vision. For some church members, doing something is the only objective. Fix the leaks; finish the bulletin on time; find enough church school teachers; keep the long-standing organizations running. Fresh vision provides the standard of purpose by which all decisions and activities are enacted.

Along the way, you will be learning specific concepts. These concepts together form the foundation of this futuring process, this intentional leaning toward your congregation's next constellation. Here is a quick look at the primary concepts that you will be using:

- Culture: human activity that is learned and shared, expressing community values and meaning.
- Declaration of vision: an appealing presentation developed and embraced by a congregation as its intended future.
- Defining functions: *the four organizational functions are "what"— programs and activities; "who"—constituents, actual and potential,*

*and their cohesion; "how"—the ways that things are done, formally and informally; and "why"—the vision.*

- Environment: all of what surrounds the congregation, whether near or far, obvious or subtle, recognized or ignored.
- Layers of culture: distinctions between communities that are based upon geographical region, history, and ethnic origin.
- Power: the ability to make things happen.
- Story: recounting a community's earlier experiences, events, and people as they become framed in a particular way.
- Theological bearings: the tools and resources from which a congregation draws its religious perspective on the journey of faith.
- Strategy: a general approach to achieving a certain goal.

Related concepts in each chapter will fill out the picture of this futuring model.

As you begin to think about this process for your congregation, see it in terms of a year-long period. Within this time frame you are seeking a healthy balance between two extremes. One extreme, the far more common one in congregations, is to come up with a mission or vision too quickly. As we will see, vision does not emerge out of simple mental assent. We who carry the legacies of the twentieth century have been instilled with beliefs in the importance of reason, order, and complex structure. As valuable as these features have been, we are beginning to appreciate in new ways the realization that human communities are not driven by reason; they live, more accurately, within culture. Logical processes and committee work can help us, but they should not become ends in themselves. If we move toward a vision too quickly, vital elements of our life and possibilities together will be missed.

In contrast, a futuring process should not drag along without a sense of direction. I doubt that this will be a problem in very many congregations, since churches that realize they need something usually proceed with an air of haste. A Christian community believes that if it truly seeks the guidance of the Holy Spirit, it will receive a calling and direction. That conviction supports the need to come to some kind of clarity eventually.

A year-long discovery of your congregation's constellation allows you enough time for several things. It helps you build a momentum of interest in the congregation rather than play into a flash-in-the-pan atti-tude. It allows you to gather various kinds of information, both within and beyond your congregation. It gives you plenty of opportunities to involve the congregation's members and groups. You also have ample time to reflect on what you are finding out and to mull over the various ideas that the findings stimulate. A year lets you establish a style within the congregation by which the fresh vision can be engaged and guided.

Futuring your church is something that no one can do alone. It takes commitment by a core of persons within the congregation, persons who exhibit authentic faith and will work respectfully with one another. This process cannot accomplish its goal without the support and involve-ment of the pastor. She or he must see congregational vitality as a pri-mary contribution of the pastoral role. She or he must help to identify and rally interested, capable church members to join this constellation team. It has the best chance of being effective when it is made up of members who represent the congregation's variety, especially in age, gender, ethnicity, and length of membership. They should be mature persons who are held in a certain esteem by the congregation as a whole. Besides discovering the fresh vision, this team will face the (sometimes daunting) task of motivating the congregation's interest and drawing it into the vision and its possibilities.[18]

Before undertaking such a venture, I suggest that you ponder the fol-lowing points:

1. Consider it carefully. If engaged properly, a constellation process will introduce some level of change. The extent of the change that can be implemented will depend in the long run upon the willingness of the congregation to be guided into the future rather than to be dominated by its past.

2. Commit to keeping the congregation informed and involved all along the way. Be vigilant about the process. Be very visible, upbeat, in-teresting, and useful. Be creative in the ways that you communicate with and enlist church members and groups.

3. Coach the process. Someone skilled in group process needs to keep things moving along, coordinating various tasks and dates, moti-vating the team, and so on. This person is to be seen *not* as the one with all the answers, but as the one skilled in leading groups toward decision.

In your circumstances, relying on the pastor or a church member may be acceptable, or engaging the services of a skilled, outside facilitator may be indicated.

4. Conduct all your team and other gatherings in an atmosphere of worship. Although congregations have much more in common with other organizations than they wish to admit, congregations nonetheless are supposed to be different. They are called by God to bear and share the good news. Worship is the church's most central symbol of its identity. So prepare to sing, read and reflect on Scripture, intercede in prayer, and use silence. You will need this to set the tone for your work together and for its outcome.

5. Commission the team in a regular service of worship. Use ritual, ceremony, and symbol to emphasize the value of this experience to the congregation. Do not simply tack it on to a convenient spot in the service, the way that some churches tend to baptize children and confirm youth.

6. Caveat: Your fresh constellation must lead your congregation to do ministry beyond itself, or it is not an authentic, gospel-driven vision. Of course, the needs of members are not to be ignored. Rather, a congregation that is meeting its members' genuine needs in a healthy manner is one that also is training and engaging them in ministry and mission. There might be occasional historical exceptions to this caveat, but U.S. churches today face plenty of opportunity for mission that can make a blessed difference.

When you are meeting together, do so in a relaxed setting that invigorates your activity: singing, praying, discussing, deciding, planning. This might be a comfortable education room, the church library, or the parlor. Use newsprint to record your deliberations, and keep the filled sheets for ready reference. You may decide to appoint as the newsprint scribe one person whose handwriting is easy to read from a distance and who is adept at summarizing the flow of conversation on the spot. Things will move along when one team member is the convener, and I strongly urge that this person not be the pastor. She or he can and should play active roles along the way, but the members of the congregation need a symbol that this futuring is about them as a church, not about a pastor's agenda.

Are you ready to begin futuring your church? Take a few minutes by yourself, and then with other church members, to think about the following:

- A highlight of your church story and why it is important to remember and pass on (heritage)
- Ten words that summarize your community *and how your congregation fits into it* (context)
- Three beliefs about faith that your congregation would not want to do without (bearings)
- "The gospel is . . . (complete the sentence)."
- "The church is . . . (complete the sentence)."

Welcome to a journey toward a faithful future.

# Heritage

## Where Your Church Has Been and
## What It Means

# 2

D O YOU REMEMBER as a child hearing stories about your family from one of its older members? Was it an aunt, a grandmother, an uncle whom you saw only on holidays? What did the person tell you? Funny stories about your parents when they were young? Accounts from "the war," perhaps of death and grief? The time he bought a new farm or opened the store, or she watched with pride as her first child graduated from college? Why do you suppose that the characters from our lineal past want us to know those stories?

Congregations have stories to tell, too. Some of them even write books about their history. I once served a church that, after 120 years, still was orally passing on remnants of its past. During my first few weeks there, several persons recited for me an account of the congregation's origins. Their accounts were remarkably similar. Together, they went something like this:

In 1872, fourteen people representing six different denominations came together to establish a union church. They came from Baptist, Methodist, Presbyterian, Episcopal, and Congregational back-grounds. It was to be a church where differences of belief were put aside. Bethany Union Church always has been a community church. Even today, our members come from thirty different religious back-grounds.

This summary reveals key qualities about the relationship between a congregation's history and its present. It shows how specific details become remembered and passed on. In the case of Bethany Union Church, its centennial history book provided accuracy for certain elements of the story. One hundred fifty pages in length, this history book is based upon careful research of church records. It notes such elements as pastoral succession, construction projects, church organizations that came and went, activities in its community, special anniversaries and celebrations, and so on. Notice in the quoted summary, however, something else besides the history. The past is linked with the present. The sense of their story is, "This is our tradition, and it still shapes who we are today."

## The Scriptures as Heritage

We are talking about heritage. Heritage is a powerful part of human experience. James Michener wrote many novels in which the stories spanned many generations, even centuries. Alex Haley wrote of his African roots. And in the Scriptures, we discover that heritage is an indispensable feature of the biblical message. Early in the Hebrew Scriptures, for instance, Joshua—who replaced Moses as Israel's leader—gathered the people at Shechem. Their bondage in Egypt was far behind them. Their wilderness wanderings—and faithlessness—had ended. They had entered, subdued, and begun to settle their tribal allotments in the long-awaited promised land. It was time for a day of reckoning.

Joshua, in his final recorded public action, called the people to listen, to acknowledge, to choose, and to mark (Josh. 24). They listened to the story of their ancestors; Joshua began with Abraham and summarized the people and events that brought them to their place of promise. He reminded them that it was through the action of God that the blessings were now theirs. The people responded. They acknowledged that what Joshua had just recited was true: indeed, Yahweh, the God of their ancestors, was responsible for their life and well-being. Joshua then called them to make a decision, to choose their god (the Israelites were constantly tempted to follow other gods that were available nearby). They chose Yahweh, their people's God. Hence, Joshua marked that decision with a solemn ceremony in which the people participated.

This "covenant at Shechem" expresses a most dramatic moment in Israel's self-understanding. It discloses the remarkable vigor that is available within a community's heritage. That vigor can shape the community's view of itself and its calling, or it can become distorted and neglected. At Shechem, the Israelites agreed that their future would be patterned after the most critical quality of their past: dependence upon the initiative of God. By claiming the story as their own, the landed Israelites positioned themselves to live into the future with faith and focus.

Joshua 24 contains one of several stories like it in the Bible. It provides communities of faith today with something of a model for understanding the potential of our particular heritages. When you read the account, you will notice that Joshua did not give in to nostalgia. Nostalgia takes heritage in the opposite direction. It takes the present situation and catapults it into the past. Nostalgia sweeps over us when we look through scrapbooks and family photo albums, when we hear a song that was popular at the time of our first date, when soldiers gather at a reunion to remember the famous battles in which they fought.

Nostalgia is not bad in itself. It serves in part to remind us that any given present standpoint came from somewhere that includes moments of meaning. Joshua certainly did not want the Israelites to forget their past. But if Israel was to understand the past, Joshua sensed that Israel needed to honor its shaping features. In that way, Israel could seek positive power for its future. It was not a matter of simply trying to repeat what happened back then, but to see how new opportunities could take shape informed by value and meaning from heritage.

A congregation's heritage holds some of the stars for a congregation's next constellation. In this chapter, you will learn a three-step process for helping your congregation to appropriate and appreciate its heritage. The goal, as implied already, is not to wallow in nostalgia, but to gain insight, understanding, and new possibilities. The three steps in this process are *hearing, interpreting,* and *projecting.* Before we see how to use these three steps, we look first at a few concepts that orient us to heritage. These concepts all relate to the general concept of culture.

## *Concepts for Understanding Heritage*

Simply stated, culture is human activity that is learned and shared, expressing community values and meaning. All human beings are influenced by culture because we cannot survive without being sustained (at least in our early years) by a community. Even persons who live alone bear the effects of cultural elements from their child rearing. Communities that create, practice, and transmit culture vary greatly in their size and complexity. We do not have to turn only to the pages of *National Geographic* magazine to observe culture, for its many forms and behaviors are everywhere. Even technology affects culture; with television, movies, and the Internet, we all are part of culture and cultures.

For our purposes here, we can think of the elements of culture in several basic categories.[1] They are (in no special order) ritual and ceremony, values, symbols, space and location, heroes and villains, and story.

### Ritual and Ceremony

Ritual and ceremony refer to actions and behaviors in which the community expects its members to participate. Rituals tend to be the behaviors done by one person, while ceremonies are designed and carried out by a group. For churches, the most obvious examples are worship and worship attendance. Weekly worship is laced with ceremony: people gathered, prayers uttered, hymns sung, scripture read, sacraments administered, and so on. Attending worship can be a ritual: we get up on Sunday morning, clean, dress, and groom ourselves, travel to the church building, enter the sanctuary, find a place to sit, and participate in the rituals that, in this case, constitute the ceremony.

### Values and Beliefs

Whatever is considered important, worthy, and desirable in a culture has some kind of value. Patterns of relationship, dress and appearance, age- and role-specific behavior, and other characteristics are endowed with value. Beliefs also are valued. They deal more with the articulation of a framework or worldview that gives credence to the life of the culture. Christian groups have common traditions and scriptures, but their values and beliefs vary—in some cases, quite markedly—from one another.

### Symbols

Symbols are things that stand for something, often abstract, and thus share in its meaning. Anything can be a symbol for someone or some culture; it all depends upon how the object/symbol comes to be associated with what it symbolizes. In North America, for instance, the United States flag usually is seen to symbolize freedom and opportunity. That same flag, however, has been burned in the United States and other places to symbolize rejection of diplomatic or military policies.

Adolf Hitler took a figure from native tribal cultures—the swastika—and turned it into a symbol of German nationalistic pride; that same figure thus became a symbol of terror to Jews and political dissidents. Swastikas that appear even today as graffiti on buildings usually do not need any interpretation. Christians have a symbol that originally had a similar contrasting meaning: the cross.

## Space and Location

When I visited Plymouth Rock a few years ago, I was disappointed. All my life, I had known "the story" of that brave band of Puritans whose Thanksgiving meal with the natives in the early 1600s began a tradition that became a national holiday. For years, I had assumed that the Rock would be a most auspicious site, inspiring appropriate reverence for courage and piety. I felt nothing like that when I stood there, looking down at the remnants of a small, nondescript boulder settled in the sand. The legend of that symbol was much larger than life.

At the same time, however, the role that Plymouth Rock plays in the mythos of the United States is universal. As we saw in Joshua 24, the Israelites' dreams became fulfilled in a place, a location. When the people agreed to follow Yahweh, Joshua led them in a ceremony that included setting up a large stone—a "witness" to their decision. There are many such spots noted in the Bible.

## Heroes and Villains

Figures in the life of a community become remembered for their significant contributions either to its health or to its detriment. The one is praised, the other condemned. National folklores include both kinds of characters. Both heroes and villains are plentiful in the Bible: hero Moses delivered Israel from villain Pharaoh; hero David slew villain Goliath; hero Jeremiah prophesied against the villain kings; and villain Saul, persecutor of Christians, became hero Paul, apostle to the Gentiles.

## Story as Culture

The recounting of a community's memories, as they become framed in a particular way, conveys important aspects of the culture in narrative form. Even today's companies develop such stories,[2] as the successes of large computer companies, for instance, demonstrate. Joshua recounted the story of the Israelites as his argument for their continued loyalty to Yahweh. The cultural power of story resides not in a thorough accounting of all possible details, but in its specific emphasis and appeal. More than a century after its founding, members of Bethany Union Church knew the salient details that formed the tapestry of its founding vision.

## Cultural Flow

Cultural flow refers to an ongoing process in which the various interacting elements of a community's culture emerge, configure, dominate, and wane over time. That is, we need to recognize that culture is not static. Even the cultures of the Egyptian dynasties and the Roman Empire changed when the long-standing, familiar political dominance crumbled. Often culture changes because of factors that it does not control, as the experiences of ancient Egypt and Rome suggest.

The same is all too true for U.S. congregations. A culture that grew to be strong and useful can lose its vitality, often unwittingly and unwillingly. A weak congregational culture is one that is losing its ability to remember and benefit from its heritage. For this reason, a congregation's return to its heritage is an important—even when painful—experience.

Keep these concepts in mind as you read the rest of this chapter, and think about how to use them with your congregation. We begin now, assuming that when you actually start, your team will be in place, well prepared and commissioned.

## *Hearing Your Congregation's Story*

What sources will give you the story of your congregation? In our era of literacy, we have the advantage of referring to records and documents when we need information. Besides looking through them, you want to talk to people, both members and nonmembers. These two sets of sources—written and oral—will provide the basis for your hearing of the story. It is a story of which you know parts, but you should be prepared to learn some new things. This can be true even when you look through church records, for sometimes our memories of events and situations are not always accurate.

## Reviewing the Legacy on Paper

Let us talk a bit more about written records, since you might suppose that they are less interesting and informative than interviews. Actually, they can reveal more about your congregation than you realize. Church records are not simply full of numbers; they also include reports from the various church organizations and governing bodies.

The statistical information can furnish your team with a feel for the trends over the years. Reports can help you get inside the pulse of the time. Minutes from church meetings, for example, often tell more of the story of an issue than *Robert's Rules of Order* requires. Finding out what was discussed and decided by the music committee or the trustees in 1959 gives you common information from which to compare and contrast for today.

Remember also that your goal is not to compile a history in the technical sense, but to discover the congregation's story and its flow. This pursuit needs to embrace not only the achievements, but also the struggles. One congregation had constructed a new facility but then ran into cash-flow problems. They stopped paying on their loan from the denomination and seemed to have been lost in the lender's shuffle. Before long, no one in the church talked about the unpaid loan.

A new pastor was called. After two years, he discovered documents suggesting to him an outstanding debt. Puzzled, he inquired of the treasurer and church officers. They had almost forgotten about it. The prospect of trying to pay it back seemed insurmountable. But their new pastor worked them through a process leading to a capital campaign. Within three years, two-thirds of the debt was paid, and the congregation's confidence had risen dramatically. "We can survive; we can be something" seemed to be the congregation's new spirit.

In this situation, the new pastor discovered a part of the congregation's story that was disabling it. Ignoring the debt eventually would make matters worse, and it was not helping the congregation's sense of accomplishment. His leadership put in motion a practical solution that gave them a victory of which they could be proud. It also changed the story. In a profound way, this church now has its own version of a death and resurrection. They are a people who can believe again, as the Scriptures say, "For nothing will be impossible with God" (Luke 1:37; see Gen. 18:14). When someone researches this church records forty years from now, there will be a vivid, significant episode to recount.

So, then, what kinds of church records should you look for? Consider this list of the more common ones:

- church bulletins
- annual congregational reports (they often include information from all the organizations and committees)
- minutes from governing board meetings
- statistical reports sent annually to a denominational headquarters
- surviving files, resources, photographs, clippings, and other historical evidence

If you have plenty from which to select over a period of decades, try to get as much basic annual information as you can:

- official membership, whether by baptism or confirmation records, family units, etc.
- average weekly worship attendance
- average weekly attendance in educational programs
- number of new members, dropped members, deaths, baptisms, and so forth
- size and structure of official organizational bodies (they often are dictated in their general form by denominational affiliation, but variation will occur locally and over time); examples: elders, deacons, trustees, governing board, committees (worship, education, fellowship, outreach, memorials, and so forth), women's fellowship and circles, bowling league, couples' club, and so forth

With a person on your team who is adept at computer work, you could even make up your own charts and graphs of this information.

Charts and graphs are not the only information that the old church records can furnish you. From the documents, you usually will be able to hear voices from the past telling of key events and outstanding figures, such as the following:

- the first service held by the founding congregation
- its first home and facilities
- construction projects and their purposes
- key accomplishments over the years

- major moments and celebrations
- tragedies and losses
- traditions that developed and were lost or maintained

Here are some of the things that you want to find out about the people:

- founding members, what they did and were remembered for
- pastoral succession
- longtime and favorite pastors, and reasons why
- members of particular note, fame, accomplishment
- unpopular leaders, and circumstances explaining why

Again, keep in mind that the goal is not simply to get as much data as you can, but to listen to the story of your church. Too much detail can distract and screen you from the story itself. Follow your leads and hunches, but do not overdo it.

### Interviewing Today's Voices

The second basic part of this listening phase is interviewing persons and groups in the congregation—and outside it, too. You will prepare sets of questions to use in your conversations. The questions that you ask persons outside the church will be different from the ones for members because the latter's experience and perception of your congregation are different.

Selection of persons to interview, both members and nonmembers, is critical to obtaining useful results. You do not want to hear the same remarks from members who have a lot of church experience in common. Instead, you will select members who represent the widest possible range of ages, length of membership, type of church activity, ethnicity and race, and so forth. Similarly, you will benefit more from hearing the remarks and impressions of a variety of persons in your community. Try not to overlap too much on individuals and the church groups to which they belong (although this cannot be avoided in smaller churches).

The size of your congregation could affect the reliability that you seek from the number of church interviews that you do. A smaller congregation probably will cover the bases adequately with around ten personal interviews and three group interviews. For a midsized church, you could do up to fifteen personal and four group; for a large congregation, twenty-five and seven probably are sufficient maximums. If you have a good grasp of the variety in your congregation, you will be able to target persons and groups that will contribute sound, beneficial information.

This process of listening to your congregation's heritage operates differently, and for different purposes, from a written survey. Surveys are often used in congregations to determine where the weight of opinion rests on certain issues and proposed projects. I have seen such survey results, in statistical form, used as leverage by church members seeking to maintain a specific position. This is a poor use of resources, especially since it does not fulfill the purpose of futuring. You are not seeking at any point in the course of constellating a fresh vision to simply find out what the people like and want. Congregational leadership has a higher calling than that. Even the listening phase must walk what sometimes may be a fine line between affirming people's experience and views while discerning the value of the views for your church's future. This insight may sound potentially harsh, yet in some circumstances, a viable future cannot be reached without it.

An exception to my recommended ban on surveys may apply to your community. Besides putting together a list of six or seven open-ended questions to ask several townspeople, your team may conclude that a brief survey of your area would be beneficial. Here your primary purpose is to find out what they know about your congregation and how they perceive it. Consider including in such a survey (as well as the interview list) a couple of questions about what they see as community concerns and needs. These responses could point in some directions that will be explored more in the next chapter, on context.

Your team can use the lists and categories presented here to help it design clusters of questions for each interview set: individual members, church organizations, and neighbors. For the *individual member* cluster, the interviews could begin something like this:

- When did you join this congregation, and what led you to do so? Why have you stayed?
- What are the ways in which you have participated? Which ones have you enjoyed the most, and why? The least, and why?

- What do you know of this congregation's history (e.g., the events and activities, the people about whom you have heard)?
- What is your favorite memory of this congregation?
- For what has this congregation stood over the years?
- If you were trying to encourage someone to visit our worship, what would you say?
- When you think about this congregation fifteen years from now, what comes to mind?

Your *church group* interviews can begin with questions such as these:

- When was your church organization established?
- What are its primary functions? How do they relate to the overall life of the congregation?
- What is the most significant contribution that your organization has made in the church?
- What would your group desire the church to be like in fifteen years, and what can your group do toward that end?

For the *community* interviews, ask,

- How long have you known about our church?
- To your knowledge, what kinds of things does our church do?
- For what is our church known in this community?
- Which five words would you use to describe our church?
- What are some local needs that churches like ours might be able to help with?
- What are your sources of information about our church?

Collecting all this information from all these various sources will take some group planning, individual preparation, and time to execute. Once your team has responses in hand, it will be ready to move to the second, and perhaps most critical, step in the heritage phase. This will involve the team in a period of careful reflection and open discussion. That second step will begin, however, in the first step because you are going to enlist those whom you interview to help you. Along with the kinds of questions listed above, you will be asking interviewees to help you make sense out of the meaning of these remembrances. This will be your purpose as you include, with the interview questions for members and church groups, questions such as these:

- When you speak of [the interviewee's answer to one of the questions], what makes this important to you? What does it suggest about this congregation?
- What makes your memories of this church so valuable, worth remembering, significant? To you? But also to the church?
- How does [something the interviewee said] express the way that this congregation is Christian?

We need to elaborate upon this step in the next section. Before we do, we leave this explanation of the first phase by reminding you that the team will need to take some time to sort through its findings. You will have hard data, from church records, and soft data, also from the records but especially from interviews. Do not be in a hurry to come to a conclusion. Your journey to discover your congregation's next constellation is not a horse race.

## *Interpreting the Story*

### Finishing the Interview

You and the team have brought together all the findings that have presented themselves to you through the above-described activities. You already have stimulated the second phase by asking church members and groups to reflect upon the meaning and importance of what they told you. For some respondents, this reflection will come fairly easily. For others, it will take some patience and prompting on your part. This especially will be true for longtime members, whose ties with the congregation run so deep that they feel that what they are telling you should be self-evident. It is your task to tease what seems obvious to them into a statement that expresses faith lived out in specific ways. The past cannot be released as a constructive force for the future if it is not named. Keeping silent about it will eventually stunt the church. This insight cannot be overemphasized, for it acknowledges the strength of a congregation's culture.

Figure 1 outlines all three steps of the story process, suggesting to your team how each step relates to the others. Team members can practice a few interpreting skills ahead of time to prepare for helping inter-

FIGURE 1

## Understanding Your Congregation's Heritage
A Three-Part Exercise to Help with Church Futuring

The purpose of this exercise is to help you draw together the stories of your congregation that you have collected and heard, in order to use them as stars for future vision. Under the LISTEN/TELL column, write down a phrase that refers to each story. Under the INTERPRET column, across from each of the first-column phrases, write a brief sentence that summarizes how you or the storyteller explains that particular story's importance and significance in your church. Under the PROJECT column, write down a sentence that you would like other members of the futuring team to consider as a way to apply each story's interpretation for the future.

|           | LISTEN/TELL<br>past | INTERPRET<br>past-into-the-present | PROJECT<br>present-into-the-future |
|-----------|---------------------|------------------------------------|------------------------------------|
| Example   | Old Mrs. Barclay always talked with kids and teens. | She wanted them to fell welcome and important as part of the church. | Church adults commit themselves to welcoming children and youth. |

When you are satisfied with your first effort at summarizing, study the relationships that you have noted. What do they suggest to you about the importance of certain patterns of behavior and relationships in your congregation? How much of a change will be called for, if your congregation takes these "projected" memories and seeks to make them strong features of your church's future? Which persons and groups in your church are most prepared to help? Which persons or groups will be hesitant or apathetic?

viewees talk about the meanings. One skill is reflected in the sample questions—asking open-ended questions. Questions that call for a simple yes or no usually do not prompt interviewees to say more, especially if they have not thought about the deeper issues for some time. Questions that allow the respondent to answer in her or his own way usually stimulate more to be shared. So does paraphrasing, an active listening skill in which you repeat in your own words what you understand the person to mean. Paraphrasing gives the interviewee the valuable opportunity to "think with a mirror," that is, to find out if you understand what he or she is trying to articulate. This one-on-one process encourages respondents to keep talking because they feel that their listener is interested.

Yet techniques alone do not communicate interest; you must be truly interested in what they have to say. The hope is that you will be motivated by your preparation and by the commitment among the team to help the congregation. The ways in which you sit, look, speak, and respond to the interviewees will communicate things to them as well. You want them to warm up to this interview because you might need to be gently persistent in it. Particularly in this step of interpreting, you want to discover more than perhaps they realize at the moment. Be prepared ahead of time to ask the "So what?" question in more than one way. Do not be afraid to say, "This might seem an obvious question, but . . . ," or something similar.

The ideal response that you are seeking about meaning goes beyond the recounted episode to a statement of its value and a theological reflection on that value. Here are some examples:

> INTERVIEWER: "This incident is important in our church because . . ." (pause)
> RESPONDER: "she helped so many people; she was a shining example of how Christians are supposed to serve others, as Jesus did."
> INTERVIEWER: "This incident is important in our church because . . ." (pause)
> RESPONDER: "he kept the church together at a time when we did not know if we would survive; he was a truly sacrificial leader."
> INTERVIEWER: "This incident is important in our church because . . ." (pause)
> RESPONDER: "they accomplished a goal that seemed beyond the church's reach; they helped the church believe that nothing is impossible with God."
> INTERVIEWER: "This incident is important in our church because . . ." (pause)
> RESPONDER: "it helped to draw the people together, to develop a strong sense of community even though we had differences."

INTERVIEWER: "This incident is important in our church because..." (pause)
RESPONDER: "it reminds me that our church realized that we were
proud of our Baptist way of doing things."

If you think of an interpretation for a particular story that you are hearing, allow your storyteller to suggest hers or his before you offer yours.
Then ask whether your interpretation makes sense to the person. In the
long run, your team aims not simply to make a few church members and
organizations feel good about being selected for a special project. The
team also wants them to become curious and motivated about looking
at the future. What better way than to "hook" them at their point of perception and then point to further possibilities?

### The Team Interprets
As I hope you can see by now, the interpreting part of the heritage phase
will begin while the interviews are conducted. By the time that the team
gathers, each one of you will have asked, listened, written, asked more,
talked, and then pondered findings from your contacts. Now you will
work as a team to perform what is probably the most decisive step for
identifying heritage stars for your next constellation. You will interpret
together your findings. This step is crucial because the usefulness of the
final step hinges on what the team does here.

In a sense, then, you are going to ask yourselves the same interpretive
questions that you asked in the interviews: Why is this feature from our
past important to remember? What should it be worth to us now? You
will be asking these kinds of questions about the stories that you have
heard, but also about the figures compiled on membership and attendance, information on church groups, the organizational structure, and
so on. If the team members have been effective in eliciting interpretive
comments from interviewees, then your work can begin there. What do
you as a team think of their "take" on the congregation's past? Is it valid?
If so, why? If not, why not? If you think it needs modifying, in what way
and to what end?

As you contemplate the team's findings, you will be working toward a
list of sentences and phrases that summarize the team's consensus on interpretation. What are the meanings from your church's past that you

identify together? You can expect to generate a list of up to fifteen of these, but do not be legalistic about this number. Three is far too few to cover the richness that your heritage represents; twenty-five is too many for most groups to work with efficiently. Your list will take shape along these lines:

Our congregation has a heritage in which . . .

- people have worked hard to express their faith together.
- individuals are valued for who they are.
- certain Christian beliefs are held high (such as _____ ).
- the members develop into an extended family.
- pastors encourage members to lead.
- giving money to support overseas mission is important.
- we adapted our worship service for changing times.
- being respected in the community is important.
- we overcame hesitation to welcome people who were different from us.
- certain families have been pillars for a long time.
- well-prepared music in worship is expected.
- conflict hurt the church.
- members gave time and money when they believed in a cause.
- children and youth are visible and respected.

In this illustration, you will notice a couple of things. First, there is some overlap in the subjects and how they are treated. That is all right; do not feel compelled to make each one look separate from the others. In real church life, interconnections are a key objective anyway. Actually, these overlaps can help your team think about your congregation in a more integrated way. This task can be especially valuable in arenas of church life that tend to be treated by themselves (e.g., building and grounds, youth ministry).

Second, a few of the illustration points are ambivalent in their value. This should not surprise your team. If you have heard and read honest accounts, then there will be episodes included that did not make the congregation's anniversary book. Financial crises that were not resolved well, the firing of a pastor, a fire in the church building, a controversy that led to departure of a block of members, improper behavior by a church leader—such events over the life of a congregation are not rare. Many times, churches do what families do: they try to ignore the situation until "it goes away," never resolving their feelings about its effect upon them.

When you uncover such situations, your job as a team is not to identify church members who are still angry and then recommend them for counseling. That would be using an individual, psychological solution for a corporate, theological problem (besides, the most angry ones might have left already). Your team might decide that the legacy of a particular piece of your church's heritage is detrimental enough that some process would help overcome its negative aftermath. Such a prospect should not be ignored or taken lightly. If your team agrees to recommend such a process to the governing board, it should consider bringing in an experienced outside person to assist.

Overall, however, your team is focusing on something else—to help your congregation see and claim stars out of its past that can be part of its constellation for the future. Once you have a list of interpretations with which your team is satisfied, you are ready to move to step three. It is a step that you will have begun to sense already, but its distinction from step two is significant. The interpreting stage dealt with the past-into-the-present; the projecting stage deals with the present-into-the-future.

## *Projecting Heritage Stars*

A temptation that church leaders seem to face almost ceaselessly is thinking about the future as basically a continuation of the past. For longtime and older members, this tendency is especially easy to understand. Their formative church years were spent supporting programs and activities that seemed stable and effective. It is thus difficult to get used to the idea that what are comfortable ways to them might not necessarily be the most faithful responses now. It is also difficult for well-established members to translate their past experiences into stars that can address a new generation of needs and opportunities. It is difficult for them to do this, but it is not impossible.

Before some readers suppose that this last paragraph belittles the church of yesterday, let me say more. We are living in a time in which change occurs at an increasingly dizzying pace. As a young adult, I welcomed many of the changes that I saw taking place. As I get older, I realize that I find myself wishing that things would slow down, that life could stay a little more familiar a little longer. Now I think that I understand more why I have heard so many older persons speak wistfully of the way things used to be. This understanding helps me to appreciate the tension in churches between a revered past and a less than certain future.

In chapter 3, we will work more with the way that change affects your church's context. There we will delve into the complexity of culture to see how the interactions of cultures present us in the church with much to consider. For the time being, we can recognize that discovering fresh vision is not the same as rearranging that with which we are most familiar. Most of the stars from your congregation's heritage might look quite familiar, but it is the constellation that expresses the vision. Even stars from heritage need the dust removed from them so that their light can shine unhindered again.

Why is this discussion important for step three of the heritage leg of the vitality tripod? Because projecting is not merely repeating. It is following meaning out of where it has been and into where it could be. Projecting translates your team's interpretations of particular pieces of heritage into an attractive possibility for your church's future. The actual change in wording, as you move from interpreting to projecting, might be minor. Yet the process that distinguishes these steps discloses a principal feature of heritage. If it is to be useful to the congregation's future, it has to be released out of the past. This might sound abstract or simplistic until your team concretely meets the inertia with which many church stories commonly tend to be identified. They are symbols of how powerfully resistant the congregation's culture can be.

Projecting heritage is an exercise in applying lived meaning to the future. The phrases that you determine in this step represent the stars from heritage that you will carry with you and use later. Let us use the sample list from the interpreting section to see how projecting works. The right-hand column in the figure (next page) represents what your team might have done with each of the sample points from step two.

In comparing the two lists you will notice the variation of relationship within the pairs. That is, the similarity in one pair may look very close, while another pair seems to diverge more. For instance, the first

## Interpreting

people have worked hard to express
their *faith together*

*individuals* are valued for who they
are

certain Christian *beliefs* are held high
(such as _____ )

the members develop into an
*extended family*

pastors encourage members to *lead*

giving *money* to support overseas
*mission* is important

we adapted our *worship* service for
changing times

being *respected* in the community is
important

we overcame hesitation to welcome
people who were *different*

*certain* families have been pillars for
a long time

well-prepared *music* in worship is
expected

*conflict* hurt the church

*members gave* time and money when
they believed in a cause

*children and youth* are visible
and respected

## Projecting

to be a church that draws people
together to express faith

to see the God-given possibilities in each person

to uphold the Christian beliefs
of _____

to create networks of familial
care and support for members

to train and exercise skills in lay
leadership

to share our resources in reaching out to others

to keep worship central and
flexible for effectiveness

to earn our community's respect
through Christian witness

to be a church where people of
all kinds are welcomed

to honor faithful service while
encouraging broad participation

to provide high-quality music
that expresses our vision

to be wise and skilled in
reconciling differences

to foster active ministry
involvement by all members

in all ways, to treat young people
as true members of God's family

pair—about expressing faith together—seems parallel; not much has changed between the interpreting and projecting steps.

By contrast, the pair about conflict illustrates the way in which your team will have to exercise judgment about projecting. If the team realizes that the church has some history of harmful stresses, its appraisal of that history is not likely going to be "Let's repeat this." Rather, it probably will agree that a constructive way to project this point has to do with learning how to work through stress and difference.

A similar contrast can be seen in the pair about music. In looking ahead, the team reasonably could affirm the value of high-quality music in worship. However, it might want to assess the issue of quality in a way that does not imply only one musical era or style. In such situations, the team will be exercising a critical role and movement—recognizing the past while not allowing it to dictate the future.

## *Engaging Your Congregation*

A task of the team all along the futuring journey is to keep the congregation interested, motivated, and active with the journey. Your team will be learning and experiencing things at a depth that few other members will share. Since the team cannot put into place a fresh constellation without the congregation, what you do with them is essential. They bear the culture, for good or ill. You need to help them get inside your team's findings and conclusions, but you cannot do so by attempting to repeat every aspect of your team's experience with the congregation. Rather, some creative approaches are called for. Otherwise, church members will not be prepared to understand—let alone to live out—the novel angles on your church's future that begin to emerge even at this stage.

No single formula offers an effective way to engage the congregation. The goal, as mentioned earlier, is to attract their interest, to motivate them to take the process seriously, and to win their confidence in your efforts on their behalf. Your challenge, then, is to design activities to increase the likelihood that the eventual goal—a shared vision—is reached.

Many congregations behave in a way that seems to assume that information printed in bulletins and newsletters will do the job. This is not the case. Cultures are not driven by reason, and running written summaries in church publications appeals primarily to mental clarity. The results of your work need to be shared with the congregation in more than one way and in situations that stimulate discussion and growth in understanding. The team will want to keep communicating the following points:

- Remind the congregation that these stars from heritage are just one of three sources for the future vision.
- Emphasize that the team is not so much seeking to create its own ideas as it is attempting to lift up an accurate mirror of the congregation.
- Encourage them not to draw conclusions yet from the list of stars, but instead to ruminate upon them.

Here are suggestions for engaging the congregation, but remember, you know what will animate your specific community of faith:

- Present occasional, brief, well-scripted conversational reports by team members in worship, summarizing progress and lifting up areas of particular importance and possible difference.
- Return to each group that you interviewed, reporting on your team's findings, its assessments, and its list of stars (projecting), and getting feedback from the group.
- Meet with all staff members, with sharing and discussion.
- Gather all the interviewed members together and hold a similar discussion.
- Include a paragraph in each weekly bulletin on one of the projected stars, explaining how it was reached and what it means to the team.
- Schedule fifteen minutes of discussion in the monthly meetings of major boards, to keep them abreast of both the process and the content.
- Ask team members to divide among them a list of key church members and make contact with each one; if necessary, practice the process that you will use and anything that you want to emphasize.

One way to test the effectiveness of your plans is to ask one another if church members are talking with one another about what the team is sharing. If not, you probably need to get some other processes going. In any case, the team needs to realize in all of its work that it is not simply going through the motions. Futuring your church is not the same as preparing for an annual bazaar or running the same stewardship campaign as last year. All the elements of your congregation's present culture will be affected in some way by the emerging constellation.

The team will run into sacred cows here and there. Sacred cows, if they get in the way of your congregation's future, will be eliminated not by reason but by shared conviction. The cultural flow of your congregation will change in some respects, and much of the congregation probably will need the team's lead to open up to such change.

If you have worked through all the parts of this heritage process, you are ready to move on to the next set of activities. These revolve around the second leg of the tripod for vitality, that of context. Because there is a great tendency for congregations to lose touch with what is around them, context is an indispensable element in futuring your church. So prepare yourselves to see the world around you in some new ways and to help your congregation understand and care about what is there.

# Context
## Being Honest about Your Church's Surroundings

TAKE TWO AMERICAN congregations, both of which were founded in 1881. Parkside made its start in the fast-paced, exhilarating life of a growing city, with its factories, streetcars, gas streetlights, baseball team, and new Victorian residential neighborhoods. Cottonwood was founded the same year as its town, on the sweeping prairie that was becoming home to more and more farmers and communities. Parkside was founded by immigrants seeking increased freedom and economic opportunity; Cottonwood was founded by the families who founded the town. Parkside first constructed a simple frame, schoolhouse-style building in which to worship, study the Bible, and hold its dinners and other social activities. So did Cottonwood. The members of Parkside urged their children to learn English well and get as much education as they could. Members of Cottonwood served on their town's first school board.

By around 1910, both congregations showed signs of prosperity. Parkside's neighborhood was filled with residents of the same national heritage; Cottonwood's town was three thousand strong with three more churches. Parkside already had outgrown its first building and was raising money for a brick facility three times the first building's size. Cottonwood was adding onto the original structure and building a parsonage. Parkside had developed an informal employment network for new immigrants; Cottonwood cosponsored a missionary couple serving from their denomination in Egypt. Both confident congregations had teams in the church men's basketball league. Their pastors were respected and active in local events.

A comparison of these two congregations around 1955 reveals more contrasts than similarities. Parkside was struggling. Membership was half its 1910 level, but attendance told even more of the story. Only one-third of the earlier numbers entered the sanctuary on a given Sunday. Few who attended did not have gray hair. Parkside's solid structure was showing signs of age and neglect.

Cottonwood's membership, in contrast, had nearly tripled since 1910. It was in the midst of another building project, this one on a three-acre lot surrounded by new houses adjacent to disappearing corn and soybean fields. Its church school classes were full. Activities were available for every age group. The mayor and even a state representative were members of Cottonwood.

By 1995, Parkside had dissolved some years earlier. The twelve remaining members averaged eighty years in age and could not afford more than a Sunday preacher who also would visit in emergencies. After selling its now-shabby facility to a growing Hispanic Pentecostal congregation, Parkside held its closing service. The local denominational executive attended and accepted the check from the building proceeds to be used as seed money for new churches.

By 1995, Cottonwood was beginning to think about repairs to its forty-year-old plant. Membership had remained steady but was beginning to age. Church school attendance was one-fourth the level of the 1950s. The female associate pastor—whose husband had a well-paying job—reluctantly agreed to reduce her workload to part-time because of three consecutive years of budget shortfalls. Her colleague had been Cottonwood's pastor for almost twenty years and was near retirement. Visitors continued to attend Sunday services nearly every week.

## What Made the Difference?

Why did two congregations that were founded the same year, that enjoyed similar early successes, that were both optimistic for many years, end up a century later in such different places? What went wrong for one and right for the other? Was there something that Cottonwood had learned how to do that Parkside forgot?

In the case of Parkside, one factor played a major, even overwhelming, role in its future. Its neighborhood changed. The post–World War II industrial boom had brought thousands of new immigrants to Parkside's city. Virtually all of the new immigrants arrived from regions of the country and world with cultures that had little in common with Parkside's ethnic background.

Parkside's neighborhood already had survived an economic disaster during the 1930s, when the depression kept enough of the older residents in their mortgage-free homes to stabilize housing stock. But the 1950s were different. Older residents were dying and their houses going up for sale. They were affordable for the new immigrants, but much less desirable for mobile middle-class buyers. By 1955, the only residents left in Parkside's neighborhood who spoke its original native language were the church members.

The picture looks quite different around Cottonwood. Its community was still growing—at times even booming. Originally a farm town, it began the sometimes painful transition into a regional center after World War II. Agricultural and light industries located there for the low taxes, clean air, public support for schools, and family atmosphere. The population tripled between 1955 and 1995, while civic involvement remained high. Forty churches provided a wide variety of ministry in the upbeat small city. Cottonwood, the town's first church, still retained fairly high visibility but was no longer the first church that new professional residents visited.

The stories of Parkside and Cottonwood could be the stories of any one of hundreds of congregations in North America. It is true that the influences affecting the prospects of any one congregation are complex. In this chapter, however, we turn the spotlight upon one such influence that is often all too quickly ignored or downplayed. That influence is context, or environment. Where a congregation locates creates parameters that both support and limit that congregation's prospects. This one simple, yet subtle and rich, observation is ignored at every congregation's peril.

Please note. Parkside here is not the bad church, Cottonwood the good one. Instead, the point is this: where your church is affects who it is and what it does. Any church that is serious about being faithful to its calling must learn to be honest about, and engaged with, its context.

## *Know What Is Out There*

When the Israelites were pursuing the promised land, they did not take on each conquest blindly, without any knowledge of the circumstances that they would meet. Instead, their leader Joshua sent out scouts as they approached Jericho (Josh. 2:1) and Ai (Josh. 7:2). Upon their return, they reported to Joshua what they had seen and heard. In the first case, the city was taken, as Yahweh had told Joshua (6:1–5). In the second case, Israel's army met with difficulty, due to some disobedience by the people (7:1–11). In both cases, the emphasis of the accounts was upon Israel's need to be faithful to divine direction. Yet both cases also involved garnering specific information about the situation that the Israelites were entering.

There is a lesson in Joshua 6–7 for congregations seeking to enter the promised land of the future. Knowledge of the environment is necessary, but it must be used wisely, toward faithful purposes. That is, seeking God's guidance is something paradoxical: know where you are going, but remember to depend upon God.

Many churches at the end of the millennium will not be effective in depending upon God because they will not take their environment seriously. In this chapter, you will learn how to do that. Congregations seeking a fresh constellation must remain in touch with the world in which they live. This chapter will raise your awareness of how your congregation's context is both similar to—and different from—what you suppose it to be. By being more aware, your team can help your congregation identify opportunities for ministry and mission that lie ahead of you, not behind you.

To get started, we will look at a few basic concepts for understanding context. These concepts are environment, hard and soft data, demographics, and layers of culture.

### Concepts for Understanding Context

The most general concept in this chapter is that of "environment." This term stands for the same phenomenon as does the term "context." By now you might have gathered something of this concept's reference. It has to do with anything and everything that is around your congregation. The environment covers broad territory. It includes things as given, such as climate and geography, as well as factors that can change, such as population characteristics. A congregation's environment takes in more than the square mile or so around its facilities. Context is complex, both obvious and nuanced, and often only partially recognized and understood.

Your team is going to study your congregation's environment; it will do so by placing the research into two basic categories. A simple way to talk of these categories is with the terms "hard data" and "soft data." Hard data represent features that can be measured and given a numerical value fairly easily. Population density, incidence of particular diseases, average days of sunshine and precipitation—these are but a few of thousands of examples of hard data. With three centuries of modern scientific investigation behind us, we have learned how to observe, gather, organize, and classify staggering amounts of quantifiable characteristics of the world. These data can be arranged and compared on graphs and charts to help us visualize something that we seek to understand.

Soft data include categories of human experience that tend to have a more qualitative character. One of the most familiar forms of soft data comes to us through interviews. When someone responds to a survey asking his or her preference of presidential candidates, the data are summarized in hard terms (i.e., x percent favor candidate A and y percent favor candidate B). When oral historians and social scientists talk with people and record their responses to questions, the data do not fit into neat, measurable categories. Yet the information can be most valuable, nonetheless, even if the way that it has to be handled is not as precise as, say, a chemistry experiment.

For your purposes, you will gather both hard and soft data. The hard data will be mostly demographic information about your community and region, which usually can be found in libraries, municipal or county offices, or an office of the U.S. Census Bureau. The demographic data that you need usually are already available, once you know where to look for the information. We will go over that part of the research a little later. Your team will design the process for gathering most of the soft data, since they are relatively more elusive. What will make them easier to find is using one more set of concepts. We refer to them as "layers of culture."

## Layers of Culture

In chapter 2, we looked in an introductory way at the notion of culture. There we defined culture and noted several of its basic elements: rituals/ceremonies, values, symbols, stories, and so forth. In this chapter, we lift up another way of analyzing culture in terms of what we could say is its sphere of influence. As your team gathers soft data about your congregation's context, it will do so by using three layers of culture. Let us consider them on a scale by size.

We will use the term "macroculture" to describe the largest of the three, the general features of which are shared among a nation of some size and diversity. A quick survey of U.S. history, for instance, reminds us that a number of characteristics are shared similarly, regardless of where one lives. These characteristics—such as individual freedom, social mobility, and participation in governance—have generated certain ceremonies, myths, symbols, "sacred" places, and so on that are identified as distinctly "United States." Add to these historic characteristics the modern phenomena of entertainment technology (motion pictures, videos, cable TV, CD players, and so forth), and the U.S. macroculture takes on an even more distinctive air. That macrocultures become imported elsewhere is not new. Neither is it new that other nations form distorted impressions of a different macroculture, based on the extent of their exposure to it. It should be troubling to American Christians, I would think, that many non-Western nations imagine the United States primarily in terms of syndicated television programming and athletic wear.

A second layer of culture is more regional in nature; it resides within a macroculture but maintains—usually for historical reasons—its own distinguishing quality. This is a "mesoculture," *meso-* being a Greek root meaning "middle." Geography and ethnicity play a big role in the emergence and existence of mesoculture. The Basques of Spain illustrate mesoculture, as does French Quebec in Canada. Regional differences in the United States have allowed several mesocultures to emerge. Without quibbling over the number or boundaries, we can recognize New England, the Eastern seaboard, the South, the Midwest, the Southwest, and the West as having their own peculiarities of culture. We even could argue that mesoculture slices across size of community: there are common cultural features among urban areas, suburban areas, small towns, and isolated rural areas. Having lived in each one of these latter four meso-cultures, I can attest to their oftentimes confusing subtlety. Since the end of World War II, the U.S. macroculture has most favored the suburban mesoculture. Whether that preference continues indefinitely remains to be seen.

Scaling down again, we reach the third cultural layer, called "micro-culture." It refers primarily to a limited geographical area—a town, rural county, or city neighborhood—but it also can describe an immigrant ethnic presence. Chicago, for instance, has been influenced by many eth-nic cultures that came with immigrants: Irish, Polish, Swedish, German, Italian, African American, and more recently, Korean, Indian, and Southeast Asian. In the midst of all this cultural richness, there is still something about Chicago that is not limited to one tradition or another or to the sum of all their parts. The Chicago microculture has its stories (the Great Fire, gangsters, development of world-class architecture, po-litical scandal), symbols (the lakefront parks, the Sears Tower, the sports teams), heroes (Harold Washington, Cardinal Bernardin),), villains (Al Capone, Richard Speck), and so on. The unique mixture of all this has created—and continues to create—Chicago's microculture.

Microculture can be as intricate as the evidence offers. I lived once in a small farming town where the main north-south street was a dividing line for three microcultures. West of that street lived virtually all whites with decent incomes and comfortable homes. East of that street lived virtually all the town's Hispanics, who had begun to give up their mi-grant work for a place to live. Their jobs paid modestly; their homes were smaller and faded; their cars were old and often dented. The immigrant families were beginning to dominate that side of town, which for some years was the only area where working-class whites could afford to live. There, white and Hispanic homes mingled, and their children went to high school with kids from all over town. Three distinguishable small-scale cultures—microcultures—existed together in that one small town. A similar phenomenon probably exists where you live.

Environment, hard and soft data, macroculture, mesoculture, and microculture—these concepts might seem awkward to your team until it has had some time to become familiar with them. Take the time that you need to understand them and how they work, for they are tools that will open doors to what you want to discover from this chapter.

## *Share the Tasks*

Since you will be collecting both hard and soft data, your team might decide to split up the tasks along those lines. Those who work with the hard data—the demographic and census material—should be persons who enjoy working with numbers. They will see a lot of them. Here is one place where you could enlist someone else in the congregation to help you. Perhaps one or two members are skilled in this area. They could do most of the research on their own, with directions and categories that you provide. The soft data work is no less challenging, even though it could be viewed as less precise. If you split up the team into two working subgroups, one person in each group will need to steer the process along.

### The Hard Data of Context

As I mentioned earlier, you can begin your search for demographic information of your community at the public library or a government office. You can even get certain census information off the Internet; someone in your church should be able get you on-line with their personal computer and take you to the right home page. Some denominational offices also keep census statistics for use by new church development projects. If you start asking, you should find your way fairly quickly.

Another source of such information is quite handy, although its subject matter and timing will be unpredictable. It would be worth the effort for one member of your team to concentrate on statistics reported in newspapers. The alert reader will be rewarded with graphs, charts, and articles on a variety of topics: population trends in the county, state, and nation; effects of aging on mobility and housing markets; changes in health care administration; differences between baby boomers and busters; and so forth. Reading your local paper with the question, "How might this affect our congregation's future?" would sensitize your team to issues close by.

Figure 2, Census Summary, outlines your hard data search. Keep in

FIGURE 2

## Understanding Your Congregation's Context

### Census Summary

A Descriptive Exercise in a Process of Church Futuring

The purpose of this exercise is to help you summarize features of your environment for which research information is available.

| | Size (sq. mi.) | Population | Age Spread | Ethnic Mix | Schools | Median Home Income | Educ. Level | Econ. Base |
|---|---|---|---|---|---|---|---|---|
| Today | | | | | | | | |
| 25 Years Ago | | | | | | | | |

Note any other information that you think is pertinent to your neighborhood or town:

When you have filled in notes for each layer, ask yourself what you have learned about your context that was not as evident to you before you began the exercise. What seems to have stayed the same? What has changed? What else would you like to learn about? How will it help you understand your context better?

mind all along that your purpose is not to see how much information you can amass, but to understand what your context is like. Several categories to be researched include the following:

- size of your area, in square miles
- population
- spread of population by age
- ethnic mix
- educational institutions
- real estate values for primary residences (both owned and rented)
- education and income levels
- economic base

You will be doing a comparative analysis between the most recent figures and those of twenty-five years ago. That is, this part of your contextual learning seeks to see what trends are taking place, trends to which you can put numbers. Do not begin by assuming that "nothing has changed much since then." You probably will be surprised by what you find. So, the census subgroup might divide the work again, between the recent data and the generation-past data. Take enough time to gather what you need, and give permission to follow a few "side trails" that look interesting.

### Name the Hard Stuff

How do you make sense out of all the demographic information that you bring together? What do you look for that might indicate special meaning and importance? To begin with, you remind your team that you seek an accurate picture of your environment. More specifically, you are watching for trends within the basic categories: population breakdowns, income, education, and so forth. If you live in an urban area, these trends shift at a pace that is noticeable within one generation. If your immediate context is less populated, trends take shape and stay that way longer, imparting a sense of permanence. Along this continuum of trends, you will find your church's situation.

One small, aging city congregation looking at its future gathered some basic information on the neighborhood where its seventy-year-old facility still stood proudly. The members knew that changes were taking place: very few of the members lived in the neighborhood anymore; most drove in from the suburbs. An immigrant ethnic population was moving in, renting modest apartments, and working at manual labor jobs. An even larger segment of the new population was the young single professional, buying up old housing stock and making major renovations to it. The trend was improving the attractiveness of the neighborhood but also beginning to price housing out of the market for families with children. It was well known in the neighborhood that many, if not most, of the single young professionals did not go to church.

The leaders of the aging congregation explained that they knew these things about their neighborhood, but they did not know if there was anything else that the church could do to reach out to them. Without coming right out and saying it, the church leaders were trying to acknowledge that the contextual trends around them no longer supported the congregation as they had known it. Instead of living with what they were discovering, they sought to solve problems in their church as they perceived them—the most obvious one to them being sources for potential new members. This focus on their congregation, rather than on exploring what kind of ministry was suggested by the data, paralyzed their futuring process. It is a common trap, one that every thriving congregation learns how to avoid.

How could this group of leaders have responded differently, to the benefit of their congregation's future? In terms of process, they could have summarized the data in the form of phrases to write on stars. Remember, stars in a constellation are not all what we *want* to see; sometimes they are what we *need* to see. Another helpful move would have been to use the hard data, and the comments that they began to articulate about those data, as a segue into the soft data. Often the hard data provide clues to the quality-of-life issues that the soft data research uncovers. Let us look at that process now.

### Soft, but Not Mushy

Your team's soft-data subgroup will use categories introduced in this chapter and chapter 2 to guide its research. It will take the three "layers of culture" categories and overlay them with several of the general culture categories from chapter 2. Figure 3, Layers of Culture, summarizes how the subgroup will organize its work.

FIGURE 3

## Understanding Your Congregation's Context

### Layers of Culture

A Three-Part Exercise to Help with Church Futuring

The purpose of this exercise is to help you understand more clearly some of the features of your environment that are harder to measure than census data. "Culture" is a very broad category describing the way that people live. Culture includes such elements and qualities as values, heroes, stories, symbols, places, ceremonies, and the like. Your church has its own particular style, but in this exercise we are looking at three layers of culture that do not depend on your congregation for their existence. Yet, in one way or another, all three of these layers affect your church.

For each of the three layers of culture listed on the left side of this worksheet, write yourself notes on important elements and qualities. Use each column heading to help you identify several of the elements and qualities.

|  | Today | 25 Years Ago | Values | Stories | Symbols | Places | Heroes | Rituals |
|---|---|---|---|---|---|---|---|---|
| Macroculture | | | | | | | | |
| *Example:* | *Freedom* | *(the same)* | *Choice* | *Amer. Revolution* | *Flag* | *Washington, D.C.* | *Lincoln* | *Fireworks* |
| Mesoculture | | | | | | | | |
| *Example:* | | | | | | | | |
| Microculture | | | | | | | | |
| *Example:* | | | | | | | | |

When you have filled in notes for each layer, ask yourself what you have learned about your context that was not as evident to you before you began the exercise. What else would you like to learn about? How will it help you understand your context better? How do you see signs of each layer of culture expressed in what your church does?

This group probably will not need to turn to many printed resources, since the answers to the questions here are part of the experience of most active persons, to one degree or another.

The easiest way to illustrate how this process works is to apply the macroculture category. The macrocultural context of all churches in the United States is that of the United States. What are some of the important macrocultural features of this country? You might agree that each member first will spend time alone working on the outline. In a few minutes, your subgroup together then should be able to make a list of many of these features. That list probably will include things such as these:

- Beliefs, for example, about freedom. (It can be helpful to explore the subbeliefs; freedom, for example, can be distinguished as political, economic, and social, and each aspect should be explored.)
- A story with key events. (Founding, sociopolitical, and economic events are often key events, such as landing at Plymouth Rock, the Boston Tea Party, Paul Revere's ride, the Constitutional Convention, the Emancipation Proclamation, two world wars, the stock market drop of October 1987.)
- Figures who made major contributions whether as heroes or villains. (Examples include Benjamin Franklin, Benedict Arnold, Thomas Jefferson, Frederick Douglass, Harriet Beecher Stowe, Abraham Lincoln, Jesse James, Susan B. Anthony, J. P. Morgan, Mata Hari, Teddy and Franklin Roosevelt, Douglas MacArthur, John and Robert Kennedy, and Martin Luther King Jr.)
- Symbols and special places. (Examples include the flag, Washington, D.C., open space and wilderness, Gettysburg, the eagle, Times Square, and white church steeples against a hillside village.)
- Rituals and ceremonies. (Examples include voting, swearing in of elected officials, shopping, graduations, attending church on Christmas Eve and Easter, and watching sporting events.)

Give your group the time that it needs to work through its understanding of what constitutes its macroculture. Fifteen minutes probably will not give you enough time; two hours should be plenty.

You will repeat this process with the other two categories, mesoculture and microculture. In both cases, it is necessary first to define the boundaries. If you live in southern California, your mesoculture is the West; if in Atlanta, the South; if near Boston, New England and the East; if in Kansas, the Midwest; and so on. What are the several features that define your mesoculture? It is a certain combination of history, geography, climate, events, figures, symbols, group practices, and so forth. Think hard together; talk freely with one another; discover the features.

You will repeat this process for microculture, and again, boundaries are significant. Is your church in rural Vermont or Dallas–Fort Worth? The two microcultures are different from each other. What they have in common is more a function of U.S. macroculture (which now includes amazing modern technologies) than anything else.

If you live in an urban area, you will have to engage the microcultural study at two levels: the metropolitan culture as a whole, and your particular neighborhood. If this sounds a bit complicated to you, I would say, "Welcome to your environment in the twenty-first century." Ministry in the next century will not be simple because the world in which we live keeps getting more complicated.

### *Mix All Ingredients and Stir*

Once your subgroups have finished their respective pieces of the work on context, it is time to come together and make some sense out of it. A tendency up to this point will have been to do the interpretation of the data as you encounter the data. As human beings, we have a need to perceive our world as having meaning. However, in this process of locating stars from context, we do not want to create closure on the picture too quickly. If we do this, we risk seeing that picture from unfamiliar or nuanced angles. Encourage one another to make notes of the ideas as you look at the data, but to keep that list of notes separate until it is time to do a full-blown rendering of them. The stars of context will emerge here.

When you are ready, then, gather the entire team and begin discussing each of the three culture lists, one by one. Let us begin with the macroculture list, since we provided a sample. From this soft data that you have collected, you will be discussing your perceptions, your understanding of this "American way" that permeates life in the United States. It is a way that is usually taken for granted, in which all the elements that make up its character are assumed. However, we live in an era that encourages questioning, a reevaluation of dominant images. This kind of questioning—at times painful—allows all of us a chance to see our macroculture in a broader framework. As we begin to appreciate the often intricate realities of U.S. history and culture, we are more able to see the same kind of intricacy at work in our own congregations. Hence, we are better prepared to acknowledge how the future might be more open-ended or different from what was first thought possible or desirable.

Your assessment process might go more smoothly and effectively if you first allow each subgroup to report on its findings and reasons for conclusions. Members from the other subgroups can ask questions to clarify what they are hearing. Once all these questions are answered, then the team as a whole can enter in, by offering comments and suggestions about wording or emphasis. In this regard, it will be important to keep in the forefront of your conversation that you are seeking your understanding through a comparison over time. Do you see trends in the demographic data? What new emphases are apparent from the analysis of layers of culture? What has stayed the same or at least maintains an appearance of stability?

One small-town church participating in a training project looked around itself and did not see much change. The town was about the same size as it had been for many years, as was the county. Its economic base, mostly family-owned and -operated farms, remained fairly strong. The church itself consisted of many longtime members, the majority being women. Through the efforts of the new pastor, the congregation was beginning to see more children and teenagers involved in activities related to the church. Several adult members stepped forward to provide further leadership for youth programming. Older members were feeling good about having kids around.

When asked what had changed in their cultural environment over the last twenty-five years, the training team members could not think of anything in particular. For them, what seemed most prominent was continuity in the midst of their lives. That team had not yet grasped the effect of macrocultural changes upon their microculture. Many cultural values and practices have shifted since World War II—family stability, role of women and minorities, levels of violence, the cost of higher education, sexual mores, television and movies as cultural influences, and so forth. For a congregation with many Depression-era adults, these changes for the most part have affected their lives very little. For the children and teens growing up in their town, however, these changes are as influential as the apparently stable microculture around them. The team was urged, then, to see its new opportunities with children and youth as a way of addressing changes for which the younger generation could use the congregation's wisdom.

This team's experience illustrates why the process of interpreting your team's findings is so important. The "So what?" question needs to be asked, both for findings that everyone expected and for those that are new (at least to some). One way to focus this process is to use an open-ended statement and fill it in with about fifteen of your findings:

"Ours is a community in which . . .

- the population has stayed steady but gotten older."
- jobs for younger adults are harder to come by."
- most people are still proud to live."
- housing values have kept up with regional trends."
- schools and other basic services are above average."
- younger residents often see public issues differently from the way that older residents see them."
- there are enough churches but not as much attendance as there used to be."
- pastors can still be community leaders."
- cultural diversity is accepted to a point."
- residents often give up instead of working together on a cause that would be good for the community."
- most of the young people who excel leave the area."
- residents are still proud of the historic buildings."
- drugs and gang activity have not become major issues."
- newcomers must live many years before being fully accepted."

Once you think you might be finished, ask yourselves if you think what you have listed creates a fair and accurate picture of your context. If the team as a whole is willing to live with the findings for the time being, it is ready to move into the final part of the contextual activities. The congregation needs to know what you have come up with, mull it over, and give you feedback.

## *What Do You Think?*

Every time you finish a leg of the vitality tripod, your basic goal is the same. You want to keep the congregation interested, motivated about what you are doing on their behalf, and willing to engage you in reflecting on the findings and insights. If you are using a visual presentation of some sort, the first thing to do is to write each finding where it can be viewed. Again, I encourage you to use the metaphor of stars and a constellation as a visual prop. Involve an artistic church member to design a wall where the stars can be written up and seen throughout the process.

Many suggestions listed at the end of chapter 2 can be used or slightly adapted here. For example, the team might decide that there are five church members whose opinions (and own learnings) would provide the team with key insights to congregational understanding and motivation. If so, it is important to prepare and undertake the informal discussions deliberately. During all parts of the constellating process, the team should be ready to deal with resistance, confusion, even anger over what it is doing or discovering. This can occur within the team itself and could undermine the eventual effectiveness of the process.

TREAT RESISTANCE NOT AS A SIGNAL TO DISCONTINUE, BUT AS AN INDICATION THAT THE CONGREGATION'S CURRENT CULTURE IS PERCEIVED AS THREATENED. Culture is not governed by the rules of rational discourse, even when we seek to use discourse as a tool for understanding. If culture, rather than reason, is at the heart of a congregation, then it should come as no surprise that resistance of some kind would surface.

When it does happen, pastoral skills are called for, but the goal is not merely to help the person feel better. In these moments, there is something for everyone to learn. Each resister has a chance to learn in a more constructive way what is important to her or him about church and faith. The team has something to learn about communicating its work effectively, looking again at its tactics. Focus should remain clearly upon benefiting the congregation's future ministry, not upon keeping certain individual members placated. At times, these two will be at odds with each other.

With this important cautionary note considered, your team should be just about ready to move to the third leg of the vitality tripod. You have identified stars out of your congregation's heritage and its context.

These stars already suggest many possible applications, some of which you no doubt have mentioned among yourselves. But the fresh constellation for your church will not arise without a third element. Heritage centers on the flow of the past, context on the flow of the present. Your future needs also to be informed by something normative, something that provides it with an orientation to what being Christian community means.

# Theological Bearings

## What It Means for You to Be God's People

# 4

## *Worth Saying "Yes"*

WHEN I WAS IN COLLEGE, I took a fascinating course called psychology of religion. It was taught by a gentle, intelligent, and well-read professor who earlier in life had served as a pastor. For the class, we students studied William James's classic book on the subject, *The Varieties of Religious Experience,* along with some contemporary works. Several of the students that semester were keenly interested in the subject out of their own deeply felt Christian faith. During most of the course, however, the professor said nothing that would give students a sense of how he personally assessed the questions of faith raised by the course.

Not everyone in the class was taking it for the same reasons. Two students were majoring in psychology, fulfilling an elective in that major (as it did also in religion). In particular, the young male psychology student in the class struck me as one feeling above the religion game; he seemed to be looking for evidence proving that religious persons had some personality weakness that psychology could explain. Neither of the budding psychologists said much in class, until later in the semester. Then, as though they had found an opening for making their point, they broached their thesis: that psychology was superior to religion. After giving them their say, the seasoned professor responded without hesitation or malice, beginning with a short statement that I never have forgotten. He said to them, "Psychology is no place for a commitment."

Psychology is no place for a commitment. What did he mean by that? I was so captivated by that simple statement that I do not remember what else the professor said to explain his point. Before I graduated, however, I learned enough from this wise teacher to confidently surmise his meaning. Psychology is no place for a religionlike commitment because it is founded upon a different premise from that of religion. By its nature as a discipline of the human sciences, psychology is not designed to call out devotion to one's experience of the holy. What is true in psychology stands in a different kind of relation to the nature of truth than do religious claims. Psychology is a tool for understanding certain arenas of human experience, but it cannot replace the religious dimension.

We live today in an era when some people would question this contrast between psychology and religion. As communities of faith, however, we look at the contrast sympathetically. My religion professor's insight about psychology's circumscribed place in the sweep of human experience prompts us believers to remember our roots. There is supposed to be something different about religion, about Christian faith, about the church, that distinguishes it from other human enterprises. Of course, there are instructive similarities between churches and other organizations; in fact, these similarities are of great interest to me. But churches need to possess self-understanding that is deeply informed by theological reflection rather than psychological or sociological categories.

This chapter explores the third leg of the tripod of congregational vitality. Dynamic congregations do not take their theological bearings for granted. Indeed, several persons have argued that the decline of mainstream Protestantism reflects its abandonment of theological faithfulness.[1] I do not want to take up this argument here. Instead, this chapter implicitly advocates what could be seen as the reverse side of the decline argument: that dynamic, healthy, growing congregations build upon a foundation that includes theological clarity and affirmation.

### *Christian Theologizing*

We find plenty of precedent for lucid congregational theology in the Scriptures. The most elaborate example might be the apostle Paul's letter to the Romans. Here Paul develops a sustained explanation of how the Christian proclamation centers on having faith in God's grace rather than on following religious regulations. In doing so, Paul draws heavily upon his Judaism, citing major figures (Abraham, Adam, David), paraphrasing texts from the Hebrew Scriptures, and through it all, enunciating a Christian theology.

A different version of Christian theology appears in Hebrews. In this sermonic letter, the author enunciates a theology thoroughly steeped in the priestly language of first-century Temple Judaism. The argument is developed that Jesus the Messiah acts on the behalf of humanity as a high priest mediates for the worshiping congregation. The theological bearing in Hebrews demonstrates more continuity with Judaism than Romans does. Yet both Hebrews and Romans express Christian theology.

The way in which Christian theology can take a variety of forms is also evident in the four Gospels. In particular, we recognize a kind of heightened theological reflection in John. This Gospel is the most different of the four: many of its episodes appear only in John; it has none of Mark's urgency; its piety feels different from Luke's heroes and heroines of true devotion; its use of the Hebrew Scriptures distinguishes it from Matthew, where many quotations are used to prove points. The picture of Jesus that John paints is more grand and cosmic than that in the other three Gospels. Yet in spite of this diversity of biblical voices, we Christians affirm the authority of them all. This affirmation underscores the pivotal role that theological bearings play for a faith community. There is a richness to Christian faith that depends in part upon its being expressed in more than one way.

## Theologizing as an Unfamiliar Task

Although every phase of discovering a fresh constellation contains its own challenge, helping your church clarify its theological bearings may become especially formidable. I say this not to promote undue apprehension among your team, but to prepare it for a journey that could contain its own road bumps and dead ends. In many of the standard-brand congregations in the United States, thinking together about God is a rare occurrence. One of the symptoms of this rarity can be seen in the small number of pastors who have been active in the last thirty years in Christian education. My data here are soft, but the impression is nonetheless a strong one. The educational ministry of too many Protestant congregations has been abysmally deficient for years. Adults have not been active in learning about their faith beyond what sixth-grade church school taught them.

The effect of this neglect of nurture has been that many church members find it difficult to articulate much of anything about Christian faith. Their biblical knowledge is rudimentary and scattered; their theology is hardly more sophisticated than that of their children; and their ability to consider life issues theologically is stunted. To the extent that this troubling summary describes your congregation, the activities in this chapter will have their own special hazards. On the other hand, this phase offers an astute futuring team an opening to develop one eventual direction of application for the new constellation.

Perhaps the biggest obstacle in uncovering the congregation's theological bearings is adult embarrassment. Many adult church members would agree at least that biblical knowledge is important to faith. If, however, a person ends up as a middle-aged member of a church and knows precious little about the Bible, what is that person most likely to do? The exceptional one will read on his or her own. Most will keep their ignorance to themselves and hope that they are never put on the spot. For many of them, even receiving an invitation to teach children's church school is being put on the spot.

Some readers might feel that these comments are much too harsh and will demoralize the team as it prepares for its work. My opinion instead is that having a sober view of your situation is not necessarily the same as being negative about it. You might be blessed, on the one hand, with a core of active church members who feel comfortable with the Bible and discussing issues of faith and life. If you are, then the immediate task at hand will be easier, yet the burden to act upon what you uncover raises the level of opportunity. On the other hand, your team might find a congregation with a generally limited understanding of— and, more challenging yet, motivation for—theology. Still, this latter scenario offers its own possibilities for exploration and education.

These thoughts anticipate some of the discussion that your team will have when it works with the following two chapters. Your focus of attention right now is upon finding out how your congregation as a whole views things theologically. Before I outline your activities toward this end, I should clarify one more premise or assumption. In some respects, it is the back side of the concern for ignorance that I raised.

This leg of the vitality tripod is identified with the assumption that Christian theological bearings exist legitimately in several forms, not just one. Especially for modern Protestantism, Christian faith is understood to have several historical streams of tradition. These streams emphasize this or that element of the Christian proclamation and prefer certain associated practices. The reason that this is the back side of the concern for ignorance is that tolerance in the public square often leads to lack of definition between the various groups. If, say, Presbyterians believe that one church tradition is as good as another, they tend to be less likely to be clearly grounded in their own way of doing faith.

Yet, in an age of so much uncertainty, clarity cries out for attention. What your team seeks for your congregation here is not so much to confront others, but to define itself. Theological bearings anchor a vital church's witness into its future. With the following activities, your team can help your church to be oriented and committed to its own bearings.

## Clarifying with Two Definitions

So far in this chapter, we have used two key terms, but we do not want to take them for granted. For our purposes, their definitions need not be long or complex, but lucid and functional. "Christian theology" can be seen as reflecting and articulating understandings of God and the world in light of the witness of Jesus the Messiah. These understandings necessarily involve dialogue with the Bible as well as with views of reality as they are encountered in life. Your team will use some of the traditional disciplines within Christian theology as categories for your application.

As I hope will become more apparent to your team, theology as such is an undertaking that is not confined to the small number of persons who get paid to do it. Anyone who claims to be Christian becomes enveloped by theology. For Christians and congregations, therefore, the question is not *whether* you do theology but *how* you do it.

The second notion already suggested is "theological bearings," a framework, a vantage point, a way of posturing within the milieu of theological options. Here, our interest is not in supposing that there is one exact and perfect way of articulating Christian theology. Simply on the historical basis of what is available, there is no one way. Many denominational traditions have been experiencing for a number of years their own versions of struggles that have been labeled with theological language.

For example, churches and pastors in search processes often want to know if the candidate is conservative, moderate, liberal, radical, or some such label, even though many of these labels do not illuminate circumstances today as well as they might have years ago. Churches today live along a spectrum of theological bearings and usually are aware of themselves in the context of the other local church options.

In this phase of the futuring process, we are interested initially in knowing how your congregation does theology. We are also interested in whether and how it seems appropriate for its theology to develop in some new or augmented way. Within the limits of this book, it is possible only to point your team in the direction of resources and options rather than to elaborate upon them. Our goal here is to help you identify the state of your congregation's current theologizing and to begin the process of discerning whether any noticeable new theological emphasis might have a place in your fresh constellation. (A little later, we will discuss how your congregation's pastor or pastors can offer distinctive leadership here.)

## *Listening to the God-Talk*

All Christians are theologians, whether they know it or not, like it or not, or are good at it or not. In hearing what your colleagues-in-theology have to say about faith, you have similar options in methods as you did in the heritage phase:

- You can develop and hand out a survey.
- You can interview members one-on-one.
- You can hold a discussion with church organizations or as an open house.
- Using something from all of these methods perhaps will serve your team most effectively.

The size of your church will influence the particular form of your approach. If your congregation is small, then more face-to-face methods might work better. If large, then at least some printed survey information likely will be necessary. Consider members who were involved with the heritage phase, and ask yourselves whether these same persons (or groups) or different ones would be better to target in this phase.

As you design your method, here are a few points to remember. First, some people will be shy about sharing their beliefs around others; yet you need to hear from them as well as from those who are eager to tell you what they think. Talkative members in a group could mislead your team toward a two-dimensional view of the congregation's theology.

Second, some of these beliefs are held dear. You might get more illuminating comments from particular persons if they have the chance to put their thoughts in writing, with the option to remain anonymous.

Third, remember that you do not have to involve every single church member to obtain the insights that you seek. As any competent statistician can explain, the sample does not need to be exhaustive for the results to be accurate.

Fourth, from a motivational standpoint, it is worthwhile to involve all persons who express interest. Individuals and groups need to be reminded, however, that just because they tell you what they think, their views will not dictate any particular outcome.

One kind of survey would consist of a list of theological statements, asking participants to respond to each one on a scale of "Strongly Agree" (5 points) to "Strongly Disagree" (1 point). Such quantification can allow sophisticated research on the set of completed forms. But to achieve reliable results, this method takes more preparation and attention to detail; you would do well to have an experienced survey writer help you. This type of survey also has the danger of feeling formal; it rarely leads to a discovery process for the congregation. If used in conjunction with other methods that allow members to express themselves, however, a quantified survey could be useful to the team.

Your team might decide that it wants to test the instrument on itself first. There would be some value in finding out the effectiveness of the wording, pacing, and sequences. If your team has developed the respect among its members that it needs, this self-test step probably would help you be more prepared and sensitized. Another possibility would be to use the instrument to predict as a team what bearings you think you will discover. This tactic could help you identify the issues to which the team wants to pay particular attention.

With these guidelines and suggestions in front of you, here are samples of two sets of questions and open-ended statements to use. You might want to introduce the activity to participants by noting that the team is looking not for "right" or "wrong" answers but for the knowledge and understanding of the participants:

Think about what you know of the Bible. Using the following biblical categories, what has been important to you in your faith, and why? Respond with as much or as little as you would like to say or write.

- verses
- images
- characters
- stories
- events
- ideas

[*Sample response:* Moses, because he followed God even when he was unsure of himself. I have had many times in my life when I did not know what to do, but I tried to do what God wanted, and I could tell in the long run how things worked out.]

Here are some terms and themes that Christians have used for centuries. What do they mean to you? What would you like to know about them?

- God
- creation
- human nature
- Jesus Christ
- salvation
- the Holy Spirit
- faith
- evangelism
- Christian life
- the church

Have any of your views on any of these topics changed over the years? What led to the change? How has that change influenced your life as a Christian?

[*Sample response:* When I was a child, I thought that God was our minister. Now I imagine God as a great spirit over all things, yet involved with all the details of life. This view of God has helped me become interested in caring about others and not just thinking about myself.]

Notice that these samples do not take long to read over, but at the same time, they cover a large amount of theological ground. Depending upon the character of your congregation, you might present these topics in a modified or expanded form. The critical issue here is to give your congregation's members the opportunity to think about, and express, their beliefs about faith in a way that your team can treat afterward.

## Listening to Unfamiliar Voices

There is another aspect to discovering theological bearings besides listening to your congregation. This aspect involves listening to voices talking about God that might not be familiar or comfortable. I refer here to the tremendous wealth of theological voices that has sprung forth in the last thirty years. Many of these voices have not made their way yet along the listening posts of our congregations. One reason for their silence in our midst is that their sources rest beyond most of our congregations' direct experience. Another reason that we have not heard them is, as I have intimated, that what they have to say forces us to examine our own lives and church life. And we usually would rather not do that.

### Newspapers, News Magazines, and Other News Media

These unfamiliar voices speak of a view of life and God with which many well-established congregations have little direct contact. This is especially the case for the thousands of middle-class, white churches that have been able to exist for years without being much affected by the distresses out of which these new theological voices have emerged. If you read the newspaper or watch the evening news, however, you know something about some of these distresses. Let us highlight some of them:

- the struggles of minority groups and persons of color to live freely, with the same opportunities and achievements as anyone else
- the poverty of millions outside North America and Europe
- the attempts by women to be treated as equals to men, in education, employment, marriage, family, and society
- the increase of homeless persons and families

- ongoing threats to rain forests, drinking water, clean air, and other natural resources
- violence in homes and workplaces and on the streets
- addictions to substances, entertainment, sex, materialism
- economic imbalances between wealthy and poor, and between developed and developing nations

All of these named distresses receive constant attention in various sectors of society. All of us know something about the problems and needs they represent. Few of us are satisfied that these troubling situations have been adequately handled. Few of us are convinced that persons garnering the ability to right wrongs are motivated at all times by sufficient compassion and wisdom.

There is a tendency, it seems, that when we recognize a massive need, we choose to ignore it or to offer a simple solution. Neither intentional ignorance nor quick fixes have a place in your team's consideration of your congregation's theological bearings. Your task at this point is not to hold a forum on all the world's problems, assuage people's consciences by talking about them, and then continue church life as before. Rather, your attention to these matters is to be undertaken with an eye toward new theological insights. Ask yourselves as a team, "How does theology look and feel to peoples whose voices in the world have been muted?"

For this step in the bearings phase, you will benefit from drawing upon outside resources. One of the outside resources you have just finished engaging: your congregation's context. "What is around you, closest to you, that needs to be addressed? Who is talking about it? Who is doing something about it?" You already have discussed these questions, to some extent, in your work on context. The questions themselves are tied to specific issues. The venture before you now is to find out how to think about the issues in theological terms.

## Theological Books and Journals

Another kind of outside resource for hearing new theological voices comes from persons who are writing about theology. Many of the books and articles are technical and complex, written by specialists for specialists. Yet you can find publications that are easier reading for lay audiences.

For example, Ana Gobledale in *The Learning Spirit: Lessons from South Africa* writes about her experiences and reflections on living as an American missionary in South Africa during the final years of apartheid.[2] The author, her husband, and their two children lived illegally in a Zulu region for seven years. In her pastoral duties, Ana came face-to-face with cruelties and injustices about which many of us can only speculate. She felt overwhelmed, angry, and discouraged by what she saw. Yet Ana reflected upon her experiences and began to see ways that she could learn. Her understanding of faith, God, prayer, truth, trust, and creative action grew from those experiences. Ana's theology was tested in a crucible of oppression; as a result, it became something new.

Another example is Tom Montgomery-Fate's *Beyond the White Noise: Mission in a Multicultural World.*[3] The author uses his personal accounts of mission work in the Philippines to reflect upon the issue of doing ministry in a culture that is not the one in which you grew up. His insights can help your team think about how it could bring theology to bear upon your church's present context.

American missionaries overseas are not the only sources of important theological reflection on unfamiliar issues. For instance, *Hope for the Mainline Church* was written by a seasoned pastor who has given years of ministry to help congregations listen to what is hard to hear.[4] Addressing the current mainstream Protestant malaise, Charles Bayer deals with mission, worship, church growth, Christian responsibility, and other topics. He helps readers to think theologically about each topic and to approach each one with a "both-and," rather than an "either-or," attitude.

For another example, John M. Buchanan writes in *Being Church, Becoming Community* about being the pastor of an old but large and growing downtown urban congregation.[5] Buchanan offers sound words of encouragement. He does not avoid the issues that must be faced in the city, but he identifies biblical and theological resources for churches seeking to find ways to respond. Both Bayer and Buchanan can help your team locate your church and stimulate your theological cogitations.

A different kind of useful resource for your team gives its readers pithy summaries of many theological concepts. *A New Handbook of Christian Theology* is like a one-volume encyclopedia, with almost 150 brief articles that cover the landscape of theology's great diversity as a new century begins.[6] Alphabetically arranged by themes, *A New Hand-*

*book* provides even the beginner in formal theological reading a good feel for the many theological concerns, movements, issues, divisions, and perspectives at hand today. Each article is concise, but provides plenty on which to ponder.

A final book to mention here—one that would help your team stretch its own theological thinking—is *Becoming a Thinking Christian.*[7] The author of this book, John Cobb, is a retired theology professor who has written several books that apply theology to weighty issues of life. In *Becoming a Thinking Christian,* Cobb seeks to help you "become aware of the beliefs by which you live and to think about them."[8] Quite concerned that many standard-brand Christians and churches have given up on doing theology, Cobb walks his readers through a number of tough theological and ethical matters. There are few books available that encourage Christians to think through beliefs and issues without spoon-feeding the "right answer" to readers. Cobb wants his book to challenge you, and his rigorous approach will help your team grow as theologians.

If your team wants to see theology being thought and applied in an up-to-the-minute format, it could look at some periodicals. For many years, the *Christian Century* has published articles on various topics that relate Christian witness to life issues—war, sexuality, business ethics, politics, and so on. Two newer periodicals with similar articles offer a more evangelical perspective—the *Other Side* and *Sojourners*. For the purposes of your team in this phase, the primary value from these periodicals would be to determine how theological thinking is used to interpret and plead a cause.

This list of books and magazines gives your team outside support for tuning in to voices that can be easy for many churches not to hear. Take some time with some of these voices, the ones that most closely fit your context. Besides seeking to understand what is heard, the team should ask itself the hard question, "How would this voice influence our church's view of Christian faith and life?" Spend enough time on this question to get past the quick and easy-looking replies.

## The Pastor as Resident Theologian

Before considering how your team will sort out all this whirl of theological reflection, we need to spend a little time reckoning with the role of your church's pastor. As I said earlier, the pastor's role in your congregation's next constellation is critical. If your pastor does not grasp pastoral ministry in terms of leadership for the future, it will be difficult for the team to create momentum that will be strong enough for lasting (congregational) effects. By this point in your team's work, I trust that you have dealt acceptably with this matter. Your pastor is in the best position to guide your way through the theological deliberations. The hope is that he or she has stayed somewhat current with theological movements, thus prepared to clarify questions and explain details.

There is another, more assertive, way that your pastor can strengthen the theological element of your futuring experience. She or he can use the pulpit and the classroom. It would provide your pastor with a creative opportunity during the year to prepare sermons with an eye focused on the theological implications of what the team is doing at any given moment. By following the weekly lectionary as a discipline, your pastor could wrestle regularly with the question "How does the meaning of this text speak to this church *as a community* looking ahead?" My experience with the lectionary suggests that in most weeks, one of the four texts speaks readily to a communal setting. The sermons do not always have to speak directly of the futuring process, yet a regular focus upon community significance will begin to sensitize the congregation.

When was the last time that your pastor taught a class? As I argued early in this chapter, adult education in many of our churches has been weak or neglected. There is a strong element of learning inherent in futuring your church. What better way to stimulate such learning than by having the pastor teach a series of courses during the year? At an introductory level, topics could include Bible overview, basic theological beliefs,[9] and your denomination's traditional doctrines and practices. Second-level courses could include a study of Amos, one of the Gospels, one of Paul's letters, one of the voices discussed above, and denominational discussions of selected topics (racism, hunger, peacemaking, homelessness, and so forth). I urge you to give your pastor the time and support needed during this futuring process to function as a teacher and theologian.

### Interpreting: Seeing Stars through These Voices

Your team has listened to the voices of the congregation as the members have conveyed their theological underpinnings. Your team also has listened to voices beyond the congregation that theologize about hard needs in the world. Your pastor has been preaching with a focus on Christian community and witness, and has been leading learning activities that develop theological skills. In the back of his or her mind, each team member has impressions of how to make sense of all this God-talk. Where do you go from here?

The way that you initially process your information will depend in part upon how much of which methods your team used to gather the information. I hope that you have resisted the temptation to gather so much data, from so many members, that the collating task by itself is daunting. The team will want a block of time devoted to the summary step itself. Employ a method of discussion that allows everyone equal access to the reported information. Agree on a way to sift through it all in an orderly manner to reduce the chances of getting lost or confused.

It will be helpful to see your task of interpreting as having two parts. First, summarize what you have gathered. Second, evaluate that summary. You might want to use some of the basic themes from the tools you used as organizing categories for the summary. What are some of the fundamental beliefs that emerge from what you discovered? Do you have a sense of why these particular beliefs are so significant? How do they affect the way that the congregation lives?

In one sense, your team will be walking on holy ground during this assessment. Theology does not have to be sophisticated to be important to those who hold it. *Do not become impatient or get in a hurry. You are engaging in an experience that probably has never been undertaken in your congregation until now.* As your discussion about your congregation's responses takes shape, you will begin to identify items that can be distinguished, such as:

- God is seen as gentle, forgiving, all-knowing, more paternal than maternal, Someone to be revered (sometimes feared?).
- Human nature is seen in some perhaps confusing ways: we can do good but we tend to act selfishly; not clear about connection between individual behavior and what governments, businesses, and societies as a whole do; see the need for salvation but not clear why.
- Jesus is recognized as Messiah, Savior; views of atonement vary: some are legalistic (God had to be paid for human sin), yet others seem to prefer a moral influence;[10] vague about meaning of divinity.

• Christian life is described mostly in personal and moral terms: pray and be nice to people; feed the hungry; and so forth.

The team probably will identify from its findings a total of about seven or so categories like this. Once you are satisfied that you have a fairly good summary pulled together, you can move into evaluation. Be sure that your team is clear about the criteria it uses for this evaluation because the criteria establish a framework for assessing the congregation's theological bearings.

One fitting criterion would be the team's interest in an unfamiliar theological voice that it believes is especially pertinent to your congregation. Perhaps young people in your community have few options for constructive activity; your team decides to bring into conversation about the congregation's bearings the cry of youth and young adults for dignity, direction, and opportunity. Perhaps prisons are close by, there is a high rate of homelessness or domestic violence in your city, or a community of new immigrants is beginning to settle in town. How can the congregation's present theological bearings be informed and even shaped by such a voice? This step of evaluation also needs time for thinking, talking, letting ideas come together, and sensing attractive possibilities.

This is the team's third and final time to lift up stars for the new constellation. Remember that in this phase you are not simply reflecting to the congregation what you found out from the surveys and interviews. You also are introducing some new theological angle or ideas for consideration. You will put together a list, as you did for heritage and context; it will look something like this:

• God, the benevolent Creator who loves the world
• humanity: can do great good but carries legacy of many evils
• the Bible, our primary guide that we study with prayer and thought
• God's special interest for people in need
• Jesus the Messiah, who supremely demonstrates God's love, forgiveness
• the Holy Spirit, God's power in our midst to reconcile, bringing hope and blessing

- the church, spiritual descendants of the biblical Israelites, called as God's leaven of hope
- God's desire that all people live with opportunity, dignity, and participation in their communities
- the importance of personal devotion in faith and as a contribution to the congregation's Christian witness

## *Keeping Information Displayed*

The phrases that your team identifies can then be written on stars and put up for display with the stars from heritage and context. In this way, the congregation can begin the process that you will undertake in the next chapter, to see a constellation forming from all the stars. By this point in the futuring process, your team should have figured out some effective ways of keeping information constantly before the congregation and stimulating their musings on what you share with them. The interest and enthusiasm should be building up now, once all the stars are out on the wall for everyone to see. Ask members to pass their insights on to members of the team. You may decide that you want to solicit comments in selected ways, too.

Being this close to finishing the central task can be both exhilarating and exhausting. Before the team moves into the work outlined in the next chapter, be sure that team members are rested and have no unfinished business from previous activities. Standing at the threshold of a fresh congregational vision can make the team feel like the Israelites getting ready to conquer the promised land: knowing the overall goal does not tell you how everything will turn out. If your team is feeling as if it is treading into new territory, it probably is. And that means that you will be discovering together a new dimension to faith.

# Futuring

## Finding Your Church's Vision

# 5

IN THE POPULAR motion picture *Rocky,* the main character is selected to box the world champion for a bicentennial extravaganza. Rocky Balboa is a washed-up young fighter, somewhat aimless, who figures that he has nothing to lose by taking the fight. His former manager rather reluctantly agrees to help him train for the bout.

As often happens in the movies, a romantic relationship helps inspire the hero, whose training and desire for the fight finally ignite. Rocky cannot help imagining what his new future might be like. His many weeks of persistence prepare his body well, but just before the event, Rocky begins to have second thoughts. He wonders if the whole idea is foolish. His self-esteem drops. The night before the fight, in a moment trembling with ambivalence, Rocky tells his girlfriend, "I just want to go the distance. I just want to go the distance."

Despite a measure of predictability and sentimentality, the Rocky story is appealing and authentic. Who is not able to identify with an unlikely hero, the character with a chance to become somebody, by preparing himself or herself for a lifetime opportunity? If Rocky had backed out of the fight, all the time and energy and preparation that he had put into it would have been for nothing. He could have told his friends what it was like to prepare for the main event, but if he had not "gone the distance," he would not have achieved what he set out to achieve.

Your team might be feeling right now a little like Rocky did on the night before the big event. You have spent several months working on three distinct sets of activities. You have gathered information, listened to many people, read reports and articles, met with one another more than you thought you would, deliberated with one another on many topics, and shared your results in several ways with the congregation. Is it still worth the fight? Are you getting cold feet? Do you believe that results will come from all this work that will be worth something?

Your team may be feeling fatigue; that is normal. If it is also feeling anticipation, then that is necessary and good. In this chapter, your focus is the fresh constellation that can guide your congregation into the future. This step in the futuring process can be frustrating, scary, and exhilarating—all at the same time. Here, perhaps more than at any other step, your team will seek God's guidance. You enter this phase trusting that the Holy Spirit is working. Discernment is more about seeing God's possibilities than determining your own interests. If you have been clothing all of your gatherings in scripture reading and discussion, singing and prayer, then you have set the tone already that your team needs to be especially acute listeners.

## Basic Concepts

This chapter has just a few concepts, although they are perhaps more complex than those of prior chapters. Vision, the primary concept, has already been discussed. Your team's main goal is to discover a working declaration of vision for your congregation. In this chapter, you will see how this declaration is sought out. The two important points are (1) that it is in progress—it can and probably will be modified—and (2) that it is more about felt conviction than reasoned statement.

Vision, we have seen already, is different from a mission statement. Mission deals with action and desired accomplishment; vision deals with a picture of the way the world could be. Vision is like the "new heaven and new earth" and "the new Jerusalem" in Revelation 21, which appear in the cosmos after Christ fulfills the *mission* of destroying all evil. A historical example illuminates the point. President Woodrow Wilson's vision of a world "made safe for democracy" led the United States into the mission of winning the Great War and then of establishing a League of Nations. If vision gets lost, then it is difficult to motivate a community when the mission itself is questioned or difficult. As the proverb says, "Where there is no vision, the people perish" (Prov. 29:18 KJV).

"Value-rationality," a term coined by Max Weber, expands on the working declaration's role.[1] Notice the two contrasting words that make up this concept. "Rationality" has to do with the way that a line of thought is used to support something. "Value" denotes worth and importance, which often are not subject to reason alone. When an organization functions on the basis of value-rationality, it deliberately has selected particular values that form parameters determining how the organization behaves. These parameters often lead the organization to do things in a manner counter to common practice.

For instance, some investors today want to work only with socially responsible companies—those whose policies promote certain positive values (environmentally safe practices and products, cooperatively owned enterprises, staying away from nations with poor human rights records, and so forth). These substantive values are the basis from which decisions about investments are made. In this case, the goal of making as much money as possible is subordinated to a stated value-rationality.

Congregations are supposed to be value-rational, too—although they do not think about it that way. What anchors a church's value-rationality is its vision, out of which the values flow. The importance of value-rationality for congregations is especially pointed because of a characteristic of congregations that can be understood with a third term.

Most U.S. congregations today function as "voluntary" associations. That is, the persons who are members of the organization choose to affiliate with it. A government or other large body does not have the power to require their membership.[2] Hence, when a nation's populace has a voice in whether it joins a church or not, a given congregation will be more attractive to individual residents if that church's value-rationality—based on its vision—is strong and clear. If your congregation is going to attract prospective members for the right reasons, it needs to have a vision worth following.

## Stars into Vision

The goal of this chapter is to take your three lists of stars and see what constellation for your church appears ahead of you. Your first list emerged out of looking back at where your church has been (heritage or past). Your second list came together from looking at where your church is situated now (context or present). Your third list highlights your congregation's understanding of what God is like in the world as well as of what other ways of seeing God at work might be most germane to you (bearings or norms). Now it is time to see the constellation take shape in the sky ahead of your congregation (vision or future).

We discussed in chapter 1 how we are associating the metaphor of constellation with the concept of vision. Vision is not the same as congregational self-image, because churches that have lost their vision still can see themselves in a particular way. However, self-image is subject to being defined almost entirely by the way that the church *has been* rather than what it *could be*. Complacent congregations have a self-image, but it is self-serving. Stagnant congregations have a self-image, but it is losing energy. Declining congregations have a self-image, but it is breaking apart. Failing congregations had a self-image, but it is like an old, water-stained photograph where the shapes and shadings only hint at what the picture actually once showed.

A congregation's vision is like a constellation because it is a picture to which the congregation looks up for guidance. Your fresh vision will not be simply about what your congregation is now, but about what it is being called to become. And it has to be appealing if it is to attract the interest, commitment, and energy of the members. Philosopher Alfred North Whitehead captured this idea well, even in his most technical work, when he said, "It is more important that a proposition be interesting than that it be true."[3] When a congregation imagines a new future, the constellation that it forms becomes for the people inviting, enticing potential. If it were realized already, it would not be vision.

This point is illustrated well in chapter 2 by the founding of Bethany Union Church. When they first organized, the charter members imagined a congregation of Protestant worshipers that would not be bound by any one particular churchly tradition. The founders came from Episcopal, Methodist, Baptist, Presbyterian, and Congregational backgrounds. They decided that none of these organizations or polities would dictate their life together as a community of faith. Instead, they would unite in a common witness to the gospel. The decision was an unusual one for the times, perhaps for any time. It provided the distinctiveness for a new congregation. Echoes of that vision have continued for a century and a quarter.

When immigrant groups settle in the United States, their churches usually are founded with a particular vision, often implicit. The vision is to offer a spiritual anchor as the first generation strives to create a new life in a strange land. The spiritual anchor is based in the native church's liturgical style, its language, ceremonies, rituals, symbols, and so forth. But it also flows easily into the social, cultural, economic, and eventually political spheres of that community's life. For immigrants, being different from the wider society creates a strong impetus for their young churches' visions.

## Moses: A Vision Represented

When Moses talked with Yahweh at the burning bush, a *vision* was being reclaimed out of the Israelites' life with God. From their *heritage,* Yahweh told Moses that the God speaking to him was the One who had a history with Moses' ancestors, Abraham, Isaac, and Jacob (Exod. 3:6). From their *context,* Yahweh acknowledged the Israelites' present condition, as slaves burdened in Egypt (Exod. 3:7, 9). From their *theological bearings,* Yahweh affirmed Yahweh's own character to Moses, with the enigmatic statement, "I AM WHO I AM" (Exod. 3:14). The vision of a people with their own land (Exod. 3:8) would be pursued by Yahweh's rescue of the Israelites from their slavery (Exod. 3:9–10, 16–17).

As Moses returned to Egypt, led the escape, listened to the many wilderness complaints, received the Ten Commandments, and struggled with his role, he was being drawn ahead by God's vision for Israel. It took faith for Moses to follow the vision, especially when the people criticized him and complained about their circumstances. It will take faith now for your team to trust that the constellating process will give rise to something that you discern as God's call to your congregation in the future.

## *Outlining the Process*

Your team will continue to benefit from the assistance of a leader for the process as well as an efficient and effective newsprint scribe. Briefly, you will be assessing the three sets of stars. Taken together, they total between twenty and forty-five phrases. You will be asking yourselves,

• What do we see in them?

- What connections and contrasts do we notice, and what conversations do we hear?
- What shape is the constellation beginning to take?

This crucial, serious, but also exciting activity will be undertaken in a meditative mood, enhanced by specific devotional practices. Once your team senses the constellation coming together, you will bring phrases together in a poetic style. By the time that you have finished with your first effort, you will have created your working declaration of vision. Then you will decide how to share this working declaration most effectively with the (by now eagerly awaiting) congregation.

As I suggested earlier, the theological term for discovering vision is "discernment." It is a lost art among many congregations, for it calls upon us to put aside our usual focus on reason. Instead, discernment is sensing the call of God, which then must be articulated. It is not that using your minds is inappropriate or worthless, but that this conscious human activity operates at the service of the leading of the Holy Spirit in your midst. I am not asking you to abandon thinking and deliberation. Discernment can be as misguided as reason can be. I am calling for you to allow the value-rationality of your emerging vision to carry the weight, even as you discuss it. For Christians believe that their congregation's value-rationality rests in the gospel. (Further help on spiritual and practical aspects of discernment for congregational vision can be found in the book *Discerning Your Congregation's Future.*)[4]

## *Engaging the Process*

Your team has gathered in its workroom. It has brought in all the stars (each one bearing one phrase or statement) that have been displayed in public view somewhere in the church building. It has at its disposal the various data, reports, interviews, and summaries that the team used to identify each set of stars. Your facilitator has reviewed the purpose of this gathering. Everyone is ready to begin.

After your opening devotional, spend a couple of minutes in silence, each team member reading over the stars; they have been set up to be seen easily throughout this entire gathering. Once members have read over the stars and refreshed their memories, enter together into a time of silent group prayer. You are seeking awareness and insight from God.

You trust that the Holy Spirit has been at work in all that the team has done up to this point. Every member has at least some idea how the stars might take shape. Now, as you sit in stillness, with images from all the various stars in your minds, you are providing the Holy Spirit with an opportunity to stimulate a common mind in your midst. The group facilitator should decide ahead of time whether to allow a free-flowing silence or to use guided imagery meditation.[5]

To allow enough opportunity for impressions, relationships, and new ideas to emerge, you should take about five to seven minutes for this meditative silence. Many of us in today's world will experience that time of silence as long. The team will benefit from this particular period of silence if it has practiced the activity in earlier meetings. You do not want members fidgeting or feeling nervous during this time. It would be much more beneficial if having become accustomed to the practice, the team members concluded this period of silence feeling as though the ideas were still coming to them.

When you conclude the silence, allow about thirty seconds for members to move out of their meditation and into a frame of mind that can interact with the others. Then it will be time to talk and listen to one another. Figure 4, Constellating a Fresh Vision for Your Congregation, can help you visualize this part of the process. Here are a few questions that can focus the early part of your conversation:

- How do stars from our heritage match or relate to our context?
- How do changes in context call for stars that match or differ from those in our heritage?
- How can we articulate our bearings in such a way that they can be heard effectively in our context now?
- Where does our heritage still connect with our bearings? Where do they branch off from each other? What does this tell us?

These questions get the team talking about how the three sets of stars talk to one another. Your tactical goal in this exercise is not simply to take all the stars as they are and arrange them in a configuration that looks good. Instead, the phrases that you seek now will emanate from the connections that you perceive between stars and sets of stars. These are the phrases from which your working declaration will be built. They will reflect the discerning that you do regarding connections between stars.

FIGURE 4

## Constellating a Fresh Vision for Your Congregation
An Exercise in Discernment of Your Church's Future

The purpose of this exercise is to help you begin to discern the shape of a compelling, fresh image of what God might be calling your congregation to become and do. Think of vision as a constellation made up of certain stars from each of the three categories below. By considering how the stars that you identified in each category might interact with each other, you will become aware of new possibilities for stars for each category with a carefully selected word or phrase.

| HERITAGE | CONTEXT | BIBLICAL/THEOLOGICAL EMPHASIS |
|---|---|---|
| (past) | (present) | (norms) |

When you are satisfied with your first efforts, study the three lists of stars. What do you hear them "saying" to each other? In what way might they be arranged to create a fresh picture that could entice your congregation for the future? Express this picture in a simple poem below, using the phrases from your lists in a creative way.

Share this poem with someone else who is participating in this futuring process with you.

## Two Illustrations

Your team probably would find it helpful to see how such conversations might actually take place. Included here are two situations, using the sample lists in each one of the previous three chapters. Let us say that someone on the team is interested in one particular phrase from heritage and two from bearings:

*Heritage-Projecting*
• to be a church that draws people together to express their faith

*Bearings*
• the church, spiritual descendants of the biblical Israelites, called as God's leaven of hope
• God's desire that all people live with opportunity, dignity, and participation in their communities

This team member begins her comments by noting that she likes what she knows about the congregation's welcoming practices in its earlier years. She wonders if the church has been as welcoming since then, but she also does not want the Christian claim of being God's people to be used as a way of leaving certain people out. She feels a strong conviction that the church should help people have good, contributing lives in the world. It bothers her that churches can become so interested in their own routines and people that they do not reach out.

Another team member chimes in, obviously animated by what he has heard. He agrees that your congregation has a tendency (he thinks that it is not on purpose) to become self-absorbed and not show genuine regard for other people on their own terms. However, he also believes that one reason for this tunnel vision is a drift away from the congregation's expression of its traditional faith. The congregation will not get excited about helping other people until it takes worship, devotion, and Christian living seriously. He would hope that unchurched people in your community would see the ways that the congregation cares for others (and he is not stuck on one way to do this) and become interested in what makes a church like yours tick.

These two team members are looking at three of the same stars but interpreting them with different emphases—one, on the outreach that the church provides; the other, on the congregation's spiritual grounding. The question at this point is not so much, "How can we make both happy?" but "Where is the call of God in this situation?" As the team talks over this apparent quandary, the facilitator's role is important. His or her job here is to help the team articulate the issues and find phrases that the team recognizes as a way to express that part of the emerging vision..

In this situation, the conversation might move to a point where the team agrees that it wants two phrases that complement each other. One might be, "Worship grounded in our heritage, seeking to speak in our own day." The other phrase then would be something like this: "Helping to improve our broken world, anchored in our corporate and personal devotion." If the team is satisfied at this point with the ideas and the wording, it moves on to another topic.

Let us also imagine an example that includes context. A colleague once told me that the pastors at her church had a vision for that congregation to be the premier mainline congregation in its region of the state. She was relating to me a clear (although somewhat partial) vision. What made this vision so useful, at least to the church's staff, was that it was located. It specified what too many churches take for granted: they are *somewhere* but not *anywhere* or *everywhere*. That is, your congregation's next constellation needs to reflect how you see it situated. If your working declaration includes no reference to your place, then it will lack the cutting edge to be something rather than anything or everything.

Let us say that another member of your team homes in on these two stars:

*Context*
• cultural diversity is accepted to a point

*Bearings*
• God's special interest for people in need

This member joined the congregation a few years ago and has been quite active. His ethnic and cultural background differs from the congregation's heritage and its current membership majority. During the work on context, he raised some questions that led to the wording of the star to which he now returns. The rest of the team know him as a person of strong faith who gets along well with others. Now as he lifts up these two stars, he says, "It seems to me that if these two stars are going to be key parts of our fresh constellation, this church needs to get more connected with our neighbors on the other side of the tracks."

Moments of silence follow. The facilitator watches for signs of response. She knows that decisions about church programming are premature at this point, yet she also realizes that this comment rests on the cutting edge of the congregation's future possibilities. An older member of the team speaks up, asking almost defensively, "We take them Christmas baskets every year, don't we?" The first member replies, "Yes, and that is an important gesture; but their needs go on for 364 more days."

The facilitator feels the atmosphere in the room tightening up. She has been waiting for a moment where her responsibility would be most helpful, so she asks the team, "What do we as a team need to come to terms with here? And what kind of statement might we develop that would express what we are trying to agree upon?" Conversation opens up. Some members remind the team of the earlier discussion about the discomfort many members (especially older ones) felt about having direct contact with poor people. Other members assert that the congregation is not racist, even though it does not attract the same amount of diversity as is present in their town. Still others claim that once people have experience being around differences, they have more confidence in offering useful help. One team member finally says, rather emphatically, "You're not going to get me to go down to that shelter."

Looking around the room at all the team members, the facilitator says, "Let's take a few moments for getting centered again." Members close their eyes and sit quietly. Then the facilitator opens up the process again. "Now, with your eyes still closed, listen to my voice as I read out loud again the two phrases that we have been discussing. Then let's meditate on them for a few more moments." She reads the phrases and sits still.

After a time, she asks the team, "What has come to your mind during this silence that you think would be helpful to this topic?" One member talks about not wanting to be made to feel guilty for not being as good a Christian as someone else. Another member speaks of growing up in poverty, working his way through college, and never wanting to feel that childhood shame again. Yet another member pleads that "we can't save the whole world." Still another member asks, "What good is it to say that Christians love others if they don't get past the barriers that everyone else sets up?"

Finally, the church's pastor speaks up. She forced herself to withhold her comments until she felt that most of the other team members had spoken first. First she offers some analysis of the conversation: "It seems to me that we are struggling here with some weighty Christian issues that are both practical and theological. Yes, one church cannot help everyone in need. Yes, Christians should not live in guilt or shame, but in the grace with which God's love surrounds us. Maybe we are having a hard time appreciating the foundation for the statement about 'God's special interest for people in need.' Maybe we think that leaves us out since we have more than enough. And maybe we feel that helping others is something that we have to do."

Sensing that the team is listening, the pastor continues, "This conversation seems to be helping us face some of the issues in the stars more deeply. Maybe our constellation needs a phrase that says something about how this congregation seeks to nurture persons firmly enough in Christian faith that they get involved with 'God's special people' out of gratitude, not guilt or duty. Does that get at what we are talking about here? Can we come up with a phrase or two that say these things?"

As the facilitator paraphrases the pastor's comments, other team members make further comments and ask questions. After about ten more minutes, they agree upon the following:

- to affirm in all our words and deeds that each person lives by the loving grace of God, as revealed most clearly in Jesus Christ
- to foster Christian growth that overflows into hands-on, and sometimes formidable, mission efforts

These two narrative illustrations have given rise to four statements or phrases that then would be woven into the first draft of the working declaration. Here are the first two:

- worship grounded in our heritage, seeking to speak in our own day
- helping to improve our broken world, anchored in our corporate and personal devotion

Your team wants to have this kind of conversation and generate these kinds of phrases. The pace and actual amount of time that you need to arrive at sufficient first-draft material will vary. You can anticipate writing new phrases, as illustrated here, but you might agree that a few of the stars can be included as you first wrote them. Expect also to spend at least a few hours on this step, because you will need that time for the sharing to produce insights and wording.

### Generating the Working Declaration of Vision

Once your team is satisfied that it has enough material for the constellation itself, it is time to compose the first draft of the working declaration of vision. You might have enough energy on the same day to work on it. You might just as likely be tired and schedule a separate gathering for that purpose. In this case, the first draft could be prepared by a subgroup of three team members. One of them should be adept with words because you are not going to write a prose piece. It will be expressed in a poetic style. Why? Because you want this working declaration to appeal, to evoke positive images and feelings, to attract and motivate persons. This is not a term paper or dissertation. Vision should be more compelling than the defense of a thesis statement.

When the first draft is ready, bring the team together again. Read it over, and ask one another questions, aiming toward the final question, "Are we ready to share this with the congregation?" When you look at it together, it should leave the team with a sense that it is more than the sum of its parts; it is more than the product of your deliberations. It is a calling from God. If your answer to this question is yes, congratulations. A lot of work is behind you. But there is more to do. The congregation needs to embrace your work and commit itself to the vision. If you have been involving the members positively all along, they are ready.

What might such a working declaration of vision look like? It is not easy to find such declarations; mission statements are more the trend these days, and they almost entirely neglect reference to context. One congregation, small and seventeen years old, developed a statement as a result of participating in the denomination's strategic growth initiative. That initiative work produced statements of values and mission as well as vision. Resurrection Metropolitan Community Church, Chicago, articulated a vision that is expressed in the last clause of its mission statement:

In the example of Jesus Christ, Church of the Resurrection MCC provides celebration and support to all people who desire a diverse and multi-racial community through worship, activities for personal growth, and ministries of service and social justice, so that society will reflect more acceptance of sexual and ethnic diversity and will seek greater spirituality, diversity and openness to all people.

Another congregation, older and much larger, also used the vision and mission categories to articulate its future constellation and direction. First Community Church, Columbus, Ohio, states its mission or its constellation to follow in this way:

First Community Church is called to embody the Gospel of Jesus Christ through the power of the Holy Spirit and the eternal love of God, honoring and expanding our heritage of innovative ministry with a commitment to growth.

To that end, we will provide:
• a center for worship, celebration, study, fellowship, and sanctuary
• resources for support for new forms for ministry
• opportunities for learning and spiritual growth through all the seasons of life
• motivation and resources for empowering service to each other and to the world
• an inclusive Christian community respecting pluralism, agreeing to differ, resolving to love, and uniting to serve.

For First Community Church, the vision emphasis is stated at the beginning, and then its implications for mission are spelled out. In spite of noticeable differences in age and size of the two congregations, these respective declarations can serve them well.

### Polishing a Work in Progress

In the final set of activities for the constellating phase, your team has an absolutely essential goal: to help the congregation (both members and active friends) understand and embrace the meaning and implications of the working declaration. The team wants to solicit feedback and insights from members and groups that will be constructive. Because the team has invested considerable time and energy in the process, it should expect that any changes suggested by congregational participation will be secondary. Changes in order and wording are most likely, both of which could adjust some emphasis. However, a team that has done its work capably has sensed the pulse of the congregation—perhaps better than it knows itself.

At the same time, your team cannot impose any working declaration upon the church. Remember, congregations—in this era and indefinitely into the future—are voluntary associations. They cannot be forced to do or be something that they do not support. Church members "vote" with their feet and their checkbooks. They choose to be involved. The entire set of tactics that you have employed throughout the futuring process to keep the congregation informed and interested is now to be fully tested. The challenge is to encourage—through their accepting the working declaration—the congregation's willing adoption of a new culture, taking shape as the declaration is followed. That new culture will look something like the current one, perhaps quite a bit, but it also will introduce new things.

The ways that you share the working declaration with your congregation perhaps will closely follow the formats that you have used already, such as initial informal visits with key opinion shapers, front page coverage in the newsletter, a special letter, reports to the official board, cottage meetings, visits with church organizations, and so forth. Notice that I do *not* recommend securing formal approval from your official board as the first step. Having the board vote right away implicitly assumes that vision and culture can be shaped by reason and formal order. As we have discussed before, churches today are beginning to realize that their lives are more influenced by the folkways of their culture than by logical processes. Eventually, the board will need to ratify the declaration if the congregation's elected leadership is to play its part in your new future. That vote, however, should be scheduled only after the team has received considerable feedback in other ways.

Even if you have been careful in communicating and listening, you should not be surprised by resistance. You likely will know well before this point where to expect opposition and what it will be. Team discussion during the declaration writing process should anticipate the resistance. Here is a significant point at which you can avoid a common mistake: concentrating on personalities. Instead, encourage the team to discuss the question "What does this resistance tell us about our congregation's present culture?" Your goal is for the congregation to move into a new future, following a fresh constellation. The opinions of individuals are pertinent only as they express attitudes toward a new culture that will either support or hinder it.

Let us follow this issue to a possible scenario. As the working declaration of vision is shared, a member here and there may be very vocal in a negative way, even threatening to quit the congregation. Do not be intimidated by such behavior. Your goal never was to find a blueprint that would keep every single current member happy. I am not promoting a cavalier or combative attitude on the part of the futuring leaders. At the same time, what is at stake is more fundamental: the ability of your congregation to follow God into the future. If your team has done its work carefully and prayerfully, the objections of a member or two do not dictate the outcome.

A colleague once served a comfortable suburban congregation. Some members were excited about a new ecumenical ministry to provide shelter to homeless persons on a rotating basis. Using the proper procedures, the group brought the request to the official board, which approved the congregation's participation. Four active, large-giving members of the church quit in protest. Within a year, however, twenty new persons had joined the congregation. When asked what attracted them to the church, they all mentioned being impressed by a church willing to become involved in community needs.

An even more dramatic example of the need to move ahead despite vocal objections is related in Michael Slaughter's account of his pastoral ministry at Ginghamsburg United Methodist Church, Ohio.[6] When Rev. Slaughter arrived at the church, he found a quaint building on an old country road. Membership was ninety. For the first two years, Rev. Slaughter emphasized his understanding of the call of God to persons and the communities they create. Some new things began to happen, and visitors showed great interest. Then a group of church members came to Rev. Slaughter. They told him that they could tell he was leading the congregation in a direction they did not favor. They would leave the congregation. Tears were shed; goodbyes were said.

Within a few more years, however, this former little country church had a weekly worship with more than 1,500 in attendance; membership was not quite as high but was more than 1,000; and the congregation offered several programs for direct-involvement mission outreach. Clearly, Rev. Slaughter's vision for the little church reflected a call from God. If the minority who objected had tried to stay and assert their will, the congregation likely would have fractured and slowly died away. New faith and Christian witness exploded at Ginghamsburg when the resistance moved out of the way.

Your team has worked long and hard. It has been careful with its charge to help find God's future for your congregation. A working declaration of vision, a fresh constellation, shines ahead in the congregation's sky. Perhaps it feels as if the work is over and everything else will take care of itself. However, to increase your congregation's likelihood of truly following this fresh constellation, there is one more step to undertake. This step is to apply the vision to the congregation as it presently functions, to evaluate and advise amendments and changes. Your team is on a roll. The concrete results are soon to follow.

# Moving Ahead

## Making Your Vision Work

THE FIFTH BOOK in the Christian Scriptures stands between the last of the four Gospels and the beginning of Paul's letters. It is a book that appears at times in the lectionary but is not often read or studied. It contains a few of the better-known stories of Christian faith: the outpouring of the Holy Spirit; Paul's calling and missionary journeys; the Council of Jerusalem. This fifth book gained a name early on based upon its main theme. It is a book of happenings, initiatives, events—the book of "the acts of the apostles."

### *The First Church Revitalization Project*

Virtually the entire account of Acts reads like an adventure novella. Something was always happening; people were doing things; there was a sense of confidence in what the figures engaged in, of urgency in getting it done. Once the mission began, the first collection of those who accepted the mission did several things together: they worshiped at the Temple, they gathered in homes to pray and shared the (now new) Holy Communion, they listened to teaching, they made sure that each follower had needs met, they incorporated new followers—and they kept giving praise to God (Acts 2:42–47).

A dash of careful attention in our reading of the Acts reveals a telling point. This new movement—the followers of the way—was a combination of fresh ideas mixed with practices from its Jewish heritage. It was both old and new. When the apostles preached, they explained the meaning of Jesus in continuity with the traditions of Abraham, Isaac, Jacob, and the prophets (3:11–26), with the familiar, defining stories of the Israelites (7:1–53), while asserting Jesus' place as the awaited Messiah (2:36). When the movement spread into Gentile territory, its leaders learned that certain ancient Jewish taboos did not apply anymore (10:1–29). They discovered, with some astonishment, that their God's Holy Spirit—which fell upon Jewish believers in Jerusalem—came to Gentiles, too (10:44–48). The reality of regularly facing situations where the old and the new blended together continued in the missionary journeys of Paul, who reached out far beyond the confines of Judea and Judaism.

For this Jesus movement to reach out beyond Judaism meant that the movement leaders had to confront questions of people and of procedures. After a certain amount of contention, it was agreed that the gospel was available to nationalities that did not share the ancient Israelite heritage. Gentiles of all kinds were welcome. Under what conditions, however? Did they have to follow Jewish regulations about food, circumcision, and the like? Furthermore, as the movement expanded, how would it organize itself to handle the various demands? One illustration of the latter question appears fairly early, when there was fussing about whether Jewish and non-Jewish widows were getting the same amount of food. The decision made then was to add an office filled by persons who would take care of such concerns (6:1–7). This action expanded the structural nature of the movement.

On the controversy over the validity of Jewish regulations for Gentile believers, a big meeting was held—an "apostolic council" at Jerusalem (chap. 15). Discussion ensued, speeches were delivered, James rendered a summation that satisfied the body, and a letter was composed to be distributed broadly. According to the narrative in this chapter, the council's decision functioned as a compromise between a narrow interpretation of their new Jewish sect and a broadly open one. In the long run, as we know, the broadly open view won out, since the Jewish version of the Jesus movement long ago disappeared. However, at the time, what was at stake can be identified not only in theological and religious terms—that is, the basis and practice of salvation through Christ. Something else was happening, too, something that anyone who has ever sat on a church committee or board has experienced. The movement had to attend to certain kinds of functions if it was to continue.

In this quick overview of the Acts, we can identify three kinds of functions, all of which need decisions: about the nature of their activity, about actual and potential constituents, and about the ways that things get done. This new religious movement described in the Acts was spurred by the vision of the Day of Pentecost, but the vision by itself would not sustain the movement. Movements do not last if they are not supported in practical, specific ways.

## The Business of Vision

Something specific and practical has to be done with your team's idea—with the working declaration of vision that after months of work and prayer you have begun to share with the congregation. If the effort of futuring your church ends with publishing the declaration in the newsletter and convincing the official board to approve it, your work will have been almost for nothing. Your team will lose most of the momentum that it has been able to stimulate along the way. Ideas do not change things unless something is done with them.

This chapter is devoted to helping your team—and, even more, congregational members—learn how to do something with your working vision and do it effectively. Both vision and action are necessary if a congregation is to share with its world a dynamic witness to the gospel. Here, we concentrate upon applying the vision so that it does not become a forgotten document; rather, we make it work for you.

At the heart of this application phase of your futuring is a simple-looking organizational model. Do not let its appearance fool you, however. The four organizational functions that we have identified—vision, activity, constituency, and procedures—provide you with a sound and practical guide for giving your futuring the feet that it needs. Your team will not quickly exhaust this model's helpfulness, for the relationships between the four functions create the tension that every organization needs to stay on its toes. Since we already have spent considerable time and effort upon one of them—vision—this chapter concentrates on the other three.

At the center of this set of activities is a key question: "From the perspective of the working declaration, what does this part of our church's life look like?" That is, you are evaluating its *current* status based upon what you have discerned as its *future* emphasis. Just as in the heritage phase—when your interpretation of stories became the pivot for projecting stars—so here your evaluation of the congregation's current conditions and qualities is pivotal. Thus, it is most crucial that these discussions are undertaken with great care and under the team's direct leadership. Whatever suggested possible actions derive from these discussions will be valuable and useful to the extent that frank assessment, clearly based on the working declaration, transpires.

A major purpose for underlining this caution is to increase the likelihood that the new ideas will be implemented. We have referred throughout this process to change, its possibility and its perceived threat. At best, a very healthy and dynamic congregation will conclude that its fresh constellation calls for minor changes. For the rest of our churches, the future must embrace some new things, such as elements in worship, new arrangements for developing fellowship, new educational emphases and opportunities, structural reorganization, and the like. The extent of any change depends, in simple terms, upon the contrast between the way things are now and the practical implications of your working declaration. Because your team cannot change the congregation's culture by itself, the work of applying fresh vision has to involve influential church members and groups in a most committed and constructive manner.

## *Prepare for the Action Process*

Here are some suggestions and guidelines to bear in mind as your team prepares to institute its action process:

1. Do not be overly concerned about how to design this phase. No one design will work best for every congregation. Your aim is to see enthusiasm for the church's future, renewed member commitment, and some level of change result. Based upon our model of congregational culture, enthusiasm, commitment, and change do not occur simply by holding meetings and voting. Eventually, these familiar processes will need to be part of what you do, but congregational culture is deeper than that. That is, do not lose sight of the forest for the trees.

2. Arrange for a team member to be present with each gathering that works on the action process. This team member should be someone who is comfortable helping to keep the gathering focused on task-

clarifying purposes, explaining parts of the working declaration, nudging the group to go beyond the surface of issues, and so forth. If the team does not have enough persons who are at ease with this role, then pair a team member with another church member who can lead group process. The two of them then should meet ahead of time to anticipate the flow of the gathering and plan how they will work together.

3. Involve target church committees, especially the ruling board. The hope is that the board's official *authority* (granted by your church's constitution) corresponds fairly well to the actual *power* that operates in your congregation. This is a distinction that your team will have acknowledged early in the constellating process and will have engaged creatively in previous phases. Certain church members and groups can have more influence than others and can sway decisions, not infrequently away from anything new. One of your team's purposes during this action process is to enhance the status of the official board in futuring. You want the board's welcome of the working declaration to reflect its role as the congregation's leader.

4. To accomplish this, the team will deploy the pastor with a couple of key team members. By this time, these three will understand the declaration well, will recognize the board's central role, and will be prepared to utilize the team's insights about your congregation's particular inertia. This inertia, closely tied as it usually is to the church's members and groups with power, becomes a guide for the team as it sets up the action structure. While the pastor and two team members monitor, interpret, and encourage the board, other team members will be doing the same in other settings.

5. Cut across typical lines of committees and communication as you organize the action groups. Be sure that comfortable friends, with common experiences and views of the congregation, are distributed among the groups with newer members whom they might not know as well. Mixing committee members across committee lines will stimulate open communication. You are trying to overcome the blind spots that are built into the congregation's current dynamics, both individual and structural. This might seem to be an insidious effort, but it is not. The entire process could flounder here if members excited by the working declaration feel that their ideas and enthusiasm cannot be channeled into positive action.

6. It is always important for church members to understand what they are they involved with and to be given helpful tools. Make their tasks and responsibilities clear. Set and follow a reasonable schedule. Create an atmosphere in which all of the groups will face the church's "sacred cows" (i.e., the aspects of your congregation that most members know have not been negotiable for some time).

7. Set an overall pace that your congregation's current culture can keep up with and that your context can bear. Both your culture and your context have to be taken into account. The more your immediate community is changing—and the more rapidly it is changing—the less time your church has to exercise all of its options. The weaker your church's culture, the more effort will be required to put the working declaration into action. Assuming that the context is somewhat stable and your culture is in fair shape, your congregation need not proceed hastily. It can take several months for the action phase to strengthen commitment, focus the plans, and prepare for changes.

With all these procedural and general preparations, you are ready to work with this chapter's basic concepts.

## *Organizational Functions*

Early in the chapter, we identified in the book of Acts four kinds of organizational functions that were evident even in the early Christian movement. Here we will give these four functions simple names and define each one.[1] Figure 5, Congregational Planning with a Fresh Constellation, capsulizes the action planning process that you will follow.

### Why
When organizations and congregations are first established, someone (or a group of someones) has been motivated by a vision of a particular purpose. Vision and purpose make the "why" function what it is. We have been using in this book the metaphor of a constellation to represent the "why" function. As we saw in chapters 1 and 5, "why"—vision—is a picture of a desired future way of being. Congregations with a clear sense of their "why" have a much better chance of remaining vital, faithful, and creative in the ways that they share the gospel.

FIGURE 5

## Congregational Planning with a Fresh Constellation

Dynamic churches are compelled by a strong sense of their identity and of God's call into the future. All decisions about *what* the church does, *how* it does it, and *with whom* flow directly out of an articulated, shared vision (*why*). Use this chart to begin applying your working declaration of vision to the other three functions of your church.

**WHY**

Write down a summary statement
of the vision or key "stars" of it.

**WHAT**

*Current*
*Activity/Program Evaluation*    *Possible Action*

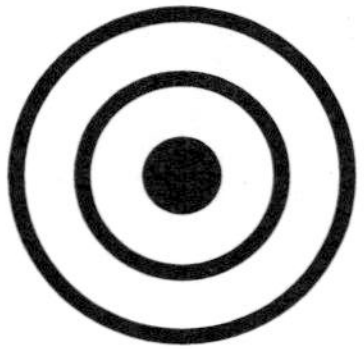

**WHO**

*Current*
*Constituencies*    *Evaluation*    *Possible Action*

**HOW**

*Operating Setup*    *Evaluation*    *Possible Action*

Plateaued and declining churches become driven by repetitious activities (WHAT) and procedures (HOW) controlled by the ethos of a membership that has become rigid (WHO). These churches eventually must rediscover a fresh constellation of vision (WHY) or they will continue to lose touch with significant ministry springing out of a vital faith.

## What

Every organization, every church, does things; it performs certain activities that it claims as basic to its existence. The basic activities for most congregations can be summarized in four categories: worship, fellowship/nurture, education, and outreach. The distinction for this function is upon what the church does, provides, and offers because of its self-understanding. A strong "what" function means that the congregation is busy and effective for its size.

## Who

Every organization and church involves people. Activities happen with, by, and for people. The "who" function deals with the congregation's constituencies, both actual and potential. It is not limited to those who are already part of the congregation, but also includes all the human relationships that touch it. These relationships include visitors, family members who are not members of that church, residents in the neighborhood, adjacent property owners, church friends, governmental bodies that can influence the church's activities and use of property, and so on. In young congregations, a strong "who" function usually means that the leaders place a high priority upon integrating prospective and new members and developing cordial neighborhood relations. In well-established congregations, a strong "who" function usually means that longtime members know one another fairly well and define the church's well-being primarily in terms of their own accustomed preferences.

## How

As an organization, a congregation not only performs certain activities and is related with certain people and communities. It also creates procedures and operations that help it use its resources with some efficiency. This "how" function occurs in two types. It has a formal shape, with committees, voting, written policies and forms, and so forth, that characterize most U.S. organizations of this era. "How" also operates informally, especially in smaller churches, where certain members are known by longtimers to be reliable for particular regular chores. When first established, procedures and operations are designed to support the programs and the people, the "what" and the "who." They are not intended to be ends in themselves. When they take on a life of their own, the congregation's culture has weakened, and most members do not realize it.

### The Functions and the Vision-Driven Church

All four organizational functions are necessary; each one has its own role to play in creating dynamic congregations. However, "why" is paramount in the sense that a church without a clear direction and calling for the future will become repetitious and drifting. "Why" is the basis for "what" and "who," since decisions about programming and constituent patrons are based upon assumptions, whether they are explicit or implicit. "How" contributes to the congregation's vitality when it makes the use of resources for "what" and "who" easier to employ. The condition of any of these four functions at any given point in time can be potent or ebbing. That is, either the function has been built up in the congregation to be active and effective, or its neglect has led to its performing a background role.

In simple terms, a dynamic congregation is one with a strong, potent vision (why), upon which active and capable programming (what) has been developed, supported by procedures (how) specifically designed to serve the programming. A vital church has nurtured each one of these three functions to be potent together, even though that means working creatively with the tension that inevitably arises between all four. The "who" function in the vital church is not dominant, however, as the other three have strength. The congregation's vision stimulates its leaders and members to reach out. A congregation that is focused clearly upon following its constellation tends to avoid creating tight networks of members that constrict access to others.

### *Plan for Action: Apply Your Declaration*

To apply your working declaration of vision to your congregation, you will follow the same basic process three times: list items appropriate to the function, evaluate them on the basis of the working vision, and then agree upon suggestions for possible action. We will begin with programming, the "what," walking through the first two steps, then doing the same for "who." Because these functions are so interdependent, your suggestions for action will be more useful if you address them after evaluating both "what" and "who."

## 1. Assess "What"

DESCRIBE

The group working on program must first put together a list of what the congregation offers. The goal is to create a comprehensive list so that it covers everything that your church does by way of ministry. This will include decisions to allow groups such as Alcoholics Anonymous and literacy training to meet in your facilities as well as programs and activities that the church originates.

You likely will discover that these programs and activities can be arranged within the four categories mentioned earlier—worship, fellowship/nurture, education, and outreach. It is not necessary to start off with these categories, however, and it might even get in the way at first. Rather, simply introduce the listing step: "What are all the ways that our congregation provides ministry? Let's be as specific as we can, filling out general observations with details. Our purpose now is to describe them." This list could shape up something like this:

*Weekly Sunday Morning Worship*
- One service, 10:30 A.M., with nursery care for toddlers and activities the second half of the service for primary-age children; average attendance over the last three years of _____ .
- Someone in the group might say, "We tried having a Wednesday night service a few years ago, but it didn't work." This comment gives your group a golden opportunity. Your purpose at this point is not to jump to evaluating or suggesting action, but to uncover reasons that explain why this program effort failed. It might have been brought up earlier, during the heritage phase. If so, the team member working with this group can fill in the others about what was learned then about the effort. Your group might conclude at this point that it was something promoted by the pastor but with little interest from board members or church members. A conclusion like this can be a valuable insight later in this step.

*Church School and Adult Study*
- On Sunday mornings during the school year, before worship (name the number of classes, age groupings, average enrollment and attendance, use of space).

*Weekly Coffee Fellowship Hour*
- Following morning worship, held in [location], providing [name the refreshments and other services], with average attendance of _____ , estimated age spreads being _____ .

*Summer Camps and Conferences*
- Vacation church school, one week, ages nursery through grade six, open to anyone in town, staffed by church members.
- Church family camp at Pine Acres, one week, trailer and tent camping open to all church members, and friends, for fellowship, R & R, with evening vespers.
- Church camp for children and youth at the diocesan-run center; eight weeks, available to several age groups and interests; we send six to ten per summer; every once in a while one of our adults will go as a counselor.

*Women's Association*
- Monthly general meetings with lunch and outside speakers (summer break).
- Six circles, meeting monthly for devotions, planning schedule for serving coffee, arranging fund-raisers.

*Youth Group*
- Sunday nights during the school year, with special summer trips; goals: recreation, increase fellowship, complement general Christian nurture.
- Service projects; led by two adult volunteer members, with pastor's help.

*Ecumenical Project*
- Representation with the Food Bank
- Homeless shelter
- Literacy project
- Occasional events

*Mission Budgeting*
- For local and denominational programs

This sample list illustrates the kinds of activities to include on your list. Again, you want the list to be complete so that it reflects all of the "what" of your congregation's current involvements.

EVALUATE

Like the challenge of interpreting heritage, this middle step must be undertaken seriously and openly if your group is to move into the third step with sound ideas. Unlike the challenge from the heritage phase, though, you now have a clearly stated benchmark from which to determine your assessment.

To open the discussion, use a question such as, "When we look at [name the item from your list] and then look at our working declaration of vision, how might we evaluate this one item?" Avoid using yes-or-no questions; they will imply that your evaluation is forced into being simply "good" or "bad." Remember, this process is not a witch-hunt. Even the most enthusiastic proponent of change in the group needs to openly recognize the benefits of activities that she or he would like to see changed.

You also may have better results if you begin with a few items that you know will be less controversial. For instance, because worship is so central to the congregation's life and culture, you perhaps should come to it later. Items such as fellowship hour and summer camping may provoke less concern. Having some satisfactory success evaluating "easier" items will boost the group's confidence and strengthen its skill in discussing "harder" items.

Eventually, the group needs to talk about the big items such as worship. Those of you on the futuring team will have realized by now that the fresh constellation for your church's future needs to be expressed positively in weekly worship. If the working declaration of vision receives a lot of hoopla, but worship continues to look, feel, and sound no different from before, the new constellation has not affected the heart of your church. Something about worship will need to be different. What it is, how much different it is, will depend upon the contrast between the character of the working vision and your church's current activities. It probably will depend somewhat upon the liturgical tradition that is part of your denomination. This point about change in worship is not necessarily a call for wholesale overhaul, however. A congregation strong enough to engage in a futuring process is capable of adjusting and adding elements to worship to give something familiar a fresh flavor.

We are getting ahead of ourselves, though, because evaluation must precede suggestions for action. Apprehension about change is always a concern with church members who are at ease with the present culture. Keeping this in mind during the evaluation step can shake the group loose from being overly protective. Even the pastor may be tempted to feel a bit defensive here. As the group facilitator keeps the basis for evaluation firmly focused upon the working declaration, the group's conversation can be fairly objective.

It may also be helpful to distinguish the various elements of worship. Typically, they include the following:

- music (vocal—choral, ensemble, solo, age groups; instrumental—accompaniment, special, traditional vs. contemporary; congregational singing—contemporary vs. traditional; selection of any and all)
- leadership (pastoral, lay, officers, youth, training, and so forth)
- the flow of the liturgy (what kinds of prayers and where; who prepares them; placement of readings and sermon, offering, special music, and so forth)
- use of scripture (decision on selection)
- preaching (content, style, purpose)
- congregational responses (doxology, prayers, offering, and so forth)

The hottest item on the list is often the role of music. Some committee members can see this as an opportunity to plead for more hymns that they like (or fewer that they dislike), different sorts of anthems by the choirs, and so on. Remember that this is not an occasion for people to simply give their opinions. They are reflecting thoughtfully upon their experience of worship to appraise it in light of the working declaration. This task indeed requires some thinking, the ability to read over the phrases of the declaration and consider worship in those terms. The hope is that the group will be able to say sometimes, "That part of the vision is supported by worship in [these ways]," as well as agree that certain parts of the vision are not yet being symbolized in worship.

One congregational team that participated in a training project lifted up in its working declaration a concern for children and youth in the community. When the team engaged other church members to assess their church life against the declaration, what was one of the questions that they had to ask themselves? It was something along these lines: "How does our weekly worship convey to all ages that this is a church seeking to minister to children and youth?" Precisely determining what shape the concern took in worship was not as important, at that point, as wrestling with the question.

Since the early 1970s, a growing number of new or young congregations have experienced dramatic increases in attendance and membership, based in no small way upon dramatic changes in worship. Many of these congregations have eliminated the classic pipe organ and traditional hymns in favor of live bands and very current, singable music. As may be surmised, most people who attend these churches are young. The style of music appeals to them, reminding us of the power of music to influence our experience of faith. We personally may not prefer a service full of such music, but that is not the point to understand here. If the working declaration of vision points to a future of meeting spiritual needs of people not yet in your church, what will draw them to you?

When you have evaluated each item that you listed under "what," you will have a mixture of both compliments and critiques. That is, your assessment should not be either blindly Pollyannaish or roundly judgmental. If anything, you can expect conclusions such as, "[This part of the declaration] is touched on by [this item], but we can see that it could be emphasized more," and "I guess that one is pretty much missing at this point." This can represent an honest and helpful appraisal. Resist with each consideration the temptation to solve the problem as you evaluate it. Ideas for step three, "suggest action," will be included in the next section.

## 2. Assess "Who"

Before moving your consideration of "what" functions to the third step, it would be a good idea to describe and evaluate "who" first. The many things that a congregation does are always linked with a target population, that is, a part of its (implicit or explicit) constituency. There is no "what" without a "who," and the value of "what" is based upon the needs of "who." One danger faced by a church is developing patterns of "who" that become rigid. Then the church's activities end up serving only the same people rather than being genuinely welcoming to others.

I have heard many congregations say they want more members. Their behavior, however, sends mixed messages. Members in such a church say, "We're a friendly church. We're here with our beautiful building, so why don't they come?" They usually are blind to seeing their underlying motivation for seeking new members: to have younger, new ones do the jobs that they are tired of doing, without making any significant changes in anything. This phenomenon is caused by the church's "who" being too tight.

This is a roundabout way of pointing to probably the major hazard facing your congregation in assessing constituency. It is in overlooking the set patterns of personal relationships, histories, influence, and decision making that already operate in your church. In themselves, these patterns are not by nature wrong or bad or evil; they likely have served the church well. Yet there is another side to their existence: they tend to create a cultural myopia that even the most benevolent church members have a hard time recognizing. The close ties that were a strength in your church's past become a weakness for its future.

Of course, a congregation should encourage its members to build good friendships and working relationships among themselves. The "who" is like the congregation's glue in the way that it can make so much happen. In futuring your church, though, this glue must stick new patterns together, not rely only on old ones. For longtime members in a congregation, this point has two practical applications. First, longtime members should develop intentional relationships with some of the newer members (which does not mean giving up their older friendships). These relationships will foster the trust needed as new ideas spun from the declaration of vision are considered. Second, longtime members should encourage the new and newer members to develop their own relationships. After all, if a longtime member is truly concerned about the congregation's future, she or he should understand the importance of some strong ties among younger members. Such ties are needed to tackle inevitable significant decisions later.

DESCRIBE

The "who" function in your church, like the "how" function, can be distinguished by both official and informal elements. It also includes members within the church and persons/groups beyond the church who have an actual or possible tie with it. The official elements involve persons and agencies such as these:

- baptized, confirmed, and other official members
- church boards, committees, women's, men's, and youth groups, and so forth
- village or city hall
- your denominational connections (usually more elaborate than most members realize or care about)
- property owners in the neighborhood of your physical plant
- cooperative agencies for which the church provides various kinds of support and improvement opportunities (Alcoholics Anonymous, Narcotics Anonymous, Boy and Girl Scouts, agencies dealing with literacy or teen pregnancy, and so forth)
- county board
- public and private schools, and any colleges
- state agencies related to property safety and use, and so forth
- the Internal Revenue Service (employment status of staff and so forth)

Informal "who" constituencies include:

- networks of relationships among church members
- the nonmember families of church members
- regular nonmember participants
- occasional visitors with no church home
- nearby residents
- persons calling for emergency assistance
- other congregations and religious groups in your area (this could be formal, depending upon your area's ecumenical relationships)

From these two lists, you can locate constituents that are both within the congregation and beyond it. With the group that is working on "who," draw up a list for your congregation, using these lists for guidance. Make it as complete as you can, which means that you also want to indicate relationships between persons and groups.

UNDERSTAND SUBCULTURE

By laying out as clear a picture of your church's constituencies as you can, you are making it more possible for your group to gain valuable insights about the phenomenon of subculture. Our main discussion of culture as a revealing category for congregations took place in chapter 2. Culture is amazingly complex, persistent, and resilient. It exists and is transmitted even among small groups of people. A "subculture," in the way in which we use the term here, describes *the variation of practices that a smaller number of persons within a larger culture undertake.* These practices express a loyalty to the culture overall (usually in some organization) and a commitment to purposes and behavior less vital to the overall culture.

This definition of subculture might seem abstract until you begin to think about the many "who's" related to your congregation. Is it not true, for instance, that subcultures emerge for the women's association, the couples' club, the youth group, the choir, and so forth? These organizations within the church arise because of ties in the congregation, yet they create certain peculiarities of value, ritual, association, symbol, and the like. That these subcultures can be at odds with one another at times is no surprise—and no secret. When the youth group wants to set up a haunted house in the church building for Halloween and use the parlor as one of the display rooms, what do you think the women will say? This room that the teenagers think of as "stuffy, old-fashioned, and hardly ever used" represents tremendous pride, tradition, and dignity to the women. The variance in the two groups' perception of the parlor rests in their different subcultures.

Such an illustration can be multiplied in numerous ways when your group begins to pinpoint all the ways that your constituencies interrelate—or not. If you are still working on the descriptive step, identifying various subcultures can be useful. Keep the focus upon determining what they look like rather than upon passing judgment on any of them or trying to figure out what to do about them.

EVALUATE

In general terms, the purpose of evaluating your church's "who" is to see the extent to which certain areas are open and others are closed. *Eventu-*

*ally, your goal for "who" is that it be fluid—that is, that the congregation develops a creative tension between having strong relationships and welcoming new persons.* This sense of floating boundary for "who is part of us" will reflect the new, emerging culture being created by your declaration of vision. Right now, you are holding up all the current "who" dynamics to the light of the declaration. Your basic question is, "How fluid are our boundaries now?" Still, you will want to ask that question in various ways, based upon pieces of the declaration.

It will take great skill on the part of the group facilitator to keep negative comments from bogging the process down. Newer members may be aware, for instance, of social slighting from longtime members that the latter either do not remember or interpret quite differently. One value of using the concept of subculture is that it frames these tense matters *in a way that diminishes focus upon individuals and their personalities.* This might seem to be using smoke and mirrors to seek the same result, but it is instead a shift of scale. Subculture can produce behavior in persons that they would not employ elsewhere. Your group can use this concept as a nonjudgmental description to talk about the life of the church, not the personalities of individuals.

Yet there likely will be challenging moments in this evaluation. Truth-naming is an important step to releasing your new constellation. But who should do it? Who in the congregation can most effectively name what is true about its windows of openness and portals of closure? To answer this question, you must remind yourselves of what you want the truth to accomplish. If you want the present culture, with its own peculiar portals, to become more fluid, the most effective way to hear the truth is from the lips of those most invested in the way that things are now. These lips belong to the longtime church members, proud bearers of a culture that will now—in their eyes—be somewhat in jeopardy.

"How fluid are our boundaries?" This question can be asked in other ways to draw out the reticence or enlighten the built-in blindness. Your group may be able to deal with the challenging side of its truth-naming if it first points out the ways that the "who" function is fairly open. Take time to highlight these points, with a question such as, "In what ways does our church already do a pretty good job of maintaining relationships?" (Remember, you have already made long descriptive lists.) Very likely, the answers to this upbeat question will open the door to dealing with the membership's rigidity. But be sure that the group feels some sense of satisfaction about the fluid aspects of its present constituencies.

Another way to expose the rigid side of "who" is to ask something along these lines: "Where in our church do the familiar and the comfortable sometimes close us off to others?" or "Where could we be more deliberate about including [name a constituency]?" These will be challenging questions for longtime members, who could feel that they are being told that their cherished groups are creating problems. In the group gathering, the facilitator will need to use judgment in sensing whether the conversation on a sensitive subject will be productive at that time. If not, then the group should agree that the issues are important enough to address in another setting.

One particular congregation had been founded some decades ago by young couples who were moving into a new subdivision of modest but comfortable homes. Now the same couples had reached retirement age; their church had not grown in years, even though their subdivision was an affordable place for new families to get their start. The church building sat prominently within the neighborhood, and most of the new families had no church home. Why was their cozy church not attracting new neighborhood residents?

There probably were several factors, but a primary one was the condition of the congregation's "who" function. The church had received very few members who had remained as long as the charter—now retired—ones. The network of families had two generations of history with one another in their church. They knew one another's joys and sorrows and shared similar experiences as a congregation. As they looked at the future, it was a challenge for the faithful, active, longtime members to know what else to try to be welcoming and hospitable. The familiarity and comfort of their "who" function came across to visitors as an invisible barrier. The close-knit group of leaders was challenged by the blind side of its constricting culture. To become successful at hospitality, the longtime members would need to become more intentional, more genuinely empathetic to visitors.

As you conclude your evaluation of your church's "who" function, you should end up with notes both of affirmation and of need. The conversation will have evoked some strong feelings and views, some of which you may have decided to explore further at a later time, perhaps in a different setting. Now you have two sets of evaluative material, one from the "what" review and one from "who." With the close dependence of these two organizational functions, your suggestions for one function likely could be shaped by the other function. What a church does must account for who is supposed to be involved. Let us, then, move to step three, suggestions for action, and consider "what" and "who" together.

### 3. "What" and "Who": Suggest Action

This step in the planning phase seems to be the one that church members usually find easiest to accomplish, especially for the "what" function. Some members in the group process probably shared their ideas while you were still describing or evaluating. However, as we have noted already, this rush to "solve" or "improve" something must be left for the last. The purpose is to allow ample time for the working declaration to be worked into the way that the congregation thinks about who it will become and what it will do. With time, candid discussion, and a full list, the group then will be ready to associate specific ideas with items.

For example, let us say that your group has evaluated your *worship life* as basically strong: the music director mixes music periods and styles, the choir enjoys the variety, prayers use familiar language, preaching includes humor and stories from everyday life, and so on. At the same time, the group identifies a generally old-fashioned feeling to worship, in light of the interests of the boomer and buster generations for contemporary spirit. The team acknowledges that the older, longtime members have the most resistance to changing present worship features. Since your working declaration specifically mentions reaching out to a new generation, the group wants to suggest constructive ways to make a single Sunday worship service appeal across the span.

This is no small task. The group probably will not come up with all the successful ideas by themselves or in one sitting. Group members may decide that one very helpful way to animate the congregation's awareness of the challenge is to hold targeted congregational discussions. Such discussions could be designed to bring together some of the church members who represent the present culture with those most committed to the nascent one. The tone of these discussions should not pit "old" against "new" but should pose the problem in a positive way, for example, "Let us look at the evaluation that the group did on worship and see what positive steps we can think of suggesting." As already noted, we know the greatest resistance is likely to come from longtime members. On the other hand, eager-beaver change agents could lose patience with the process, alienating those whose influence is necessary to change the culture. Thus, both camps need patience and understanding.

Through discussion, such a gathering might agree that certain specific changes can be recommended on a trial basis, for a period of at least six months. The reasons for the changes would be clearly explained in the newsletter and bulletin and from the pulpit some weeks ahead in worship. Evaluation of the changes would be conducted the same way that evaluation of the current service was conducted: in light of the working declaration of vision. Church members will agree not to use gossip as a way to undermine the trial; rather, they will use their formal (i.e., committee positions) and informal networks (church friendships) to explain the trial and promote willing participation.

For certain other items from the "what" list, the group may be able to agree on some recommendations for fairly immediate action. For instance, if the declaration calls forth a membership well grounded in Bible, theology, and spiritual practice, the group may recommend that another *adult study* be added at a time when the target group is able to participate.[2] If the declaration speaks of a congregation embracing the generations, the group may recommend that *intergenerational fellowship* and educational activities become a priority. Similarly, new vision for expanding *direct mission* engagement may lead to a suggestion that the standing mission committee prioritize the congregation's mission commitments on the basis of increased hands-on opportunities.

Let us now also consider an example from a hypothetical "who" list. Let us say that your group evaluated *the relationship between longtime members and newcomers*. It was a strenuous discussion, but you reached an understanding that each group (i.e., subculture) was cordial but somewhat suspicious of the other. Longtime members acknowledged that newcomers were friendly, talented, and energetic but also voiced concern that newcomers did not respect enough of the traditions. Newcomers did not understand the set ways; they wanted to change more than the longtimers would like. For their part, newcomers reported feeling politely welcomed at first but kind of lost in the maze of activities after they joined. They admitted being less attached to certain church practices; yet they also articulated more interest in the church being able to continue attracting others with what it has to offer. This scenario is fairly common. What possible suggestions for action may be effective?

First, remember again your focus: the future as you see it through the constellation of your declaration of vision. That future will express, in most cases, a working tension between the way things have been and the way they could be. The past does have a contribution to make, although never in quite the form that those who cherish the past remember it. This way of framing the congregation's movement into the future seeks to avoid creating solutions that are "either-or," with a winner and a loser. Rather, a "both-and" perspective helps all parties realize that in the future, everyone wins some and loses some.

One suggestion for action that the group might agree to pursue would be a "clan fellowship" project. Its purpose would be to increase and broaden the network of relationships between longtimers and newer members. Secondarily, then, this broadened network would smooth the way for better mutual support, for cooperation in church organizations, and hence for significant decisions that the congregation will face in the near future. Newcomers would be seen as outsiders being adopted into the congregational "clan" by the longtimers. Their lives and contributions will be more valued and useful as they become better known.

In turn, longtimers would be seen as the bearers of the traditions and stories that represent potency even for the future. These significant symbols will be passed on, respectfully but not uncritically, as longtime and newer members trust and share experiences with each other. Because a clan fellowship project would be intentional, it could combine new twists on annual congregational events with a couple of new events aimed specifically at the project's purposes. Church dinners could include a seating arrangement and table activities designed to learn a little more about one another and have fun. Seasonal events in Advent, Pentecost, or Lent could be set up to deliberately enrich each subculture through favorable interaction with the other.

These suggestions should stimulate your group's creativity. When church members begin to get the hang of using the declaration of vision to describe, evaluate, and suggest ideas, good things can happen. As you may have guessed by now, there is no set outcome for this process. You want it to be authentically linked to the working declaration, to hold positive potential, and to motivate more members to think about your future in creative, constructive ways. This same statement can be made for the outcome from the "how" process, although the focus of subject will be different for it. Let us proceed to consider how this same process can help your congregation modify or redefine the structures and processes that are supposed to assist its life and ministry.

## 4. Assess "How"

We all have heard the saying that someone has "put the cart before the horse." This metaphor describes a common pitfall of well-established congregations. The purpose of the horse is to pull the cart where you want it to go. The reverse will not work: the cart cannot perform the same function that the horse does. Perhaps this is overstating the obvious, but carts and horses get mixed up at times in the lives of congregations.

Churches that have been losing members for years cling to an organizational structure that increasingly preoccupies their time and energy. For what purposes was that structure created? Originally, it was to serve the programming (what) and people (who), the heart of its ministry. Yet when committees, processes, and structures take on lives of their own, the vitality of that church's ministry begins to suffer.

That is, "how's" sole purpose is to make easier and better the "what" and "who" of the congregation's life. When "what" and "who" are based upon a faithful, strong, engaging constellation (why), the congregation is in its prime. Visually, then, the four functions create a diamond shape, with "why" on top, "what" and "who" across from each other, and "how" underneath them all. The energy for the dynamics, however, flows from "why" to "what" and "who" and from there to "how." When these flows of energy reverse, the congregation is in trouble.

DESCRIBE

The first thing to do is to make a list of every official and informal "how" in your congregation. If your church is small, the informal category may be the longer of the two. If your church is large, it perhaps will be the other way around. What is important at this point is to become aware of all the ways that the "how" function is present in your congregation.

The organizational structure of your church defines the official aspect of its "how." It might look like this:

- Church Council
- Board of Deacons
- Committees: Mission, Education, Fellowship, Property and Finance, Stewardship, and so forth
- Women's Association and circles

Within committees and boards, substructures are often developed to oversee that organization's activities. The Mission Committee, for instance, could be divided into denominational, local, ecumenical, and special offerings. Educational ministries could be distributed between groups that concentrate on church school, adult learning, youth groups, camps and conferences, and so forth. The influence of modern bureaucratic organizational processes is evident here. Their goal has been to make specialized tasks more efficient. In many denominational traditions, this model was adopted decades ago without question.

We know, though, that there is also an informal side to the ways that things are done in our congregations. The official structures do not always function the way that they are intended to function. It takes some measure of deliberate effort for a congregation to stick with formal procedures, especially when you know that it would be faster to ask John and Fred to work on the boiler or Lena to arrange nursery care for the annual dinner. A congregation's denominational polity will dictate to a certain degree the flexibility of the local church in structures and procedures. Yet even these parameters can be worked around in certain situations and to some extent.

Every congregation's list of informal "how" functions will be idiosyncratic, that is, quite specific to its circumstances and history. Yours will look something like this:

- John and Sue Grafton will build sets and props for church plays.
- Sandra Lathon and Jim Williams always volunteer to accompany children on field trips.
- The church secretary will help in the kitchen during church dinners, even though it is not in her position description.

• Bob Kerr always checks lights and doors and locks the church at night.
• Sam Rutkowski keeps lighting and wiring in the church building up-to-date.

Calling these activities part of the informal side of "how" does not demean them. Longtime church members have been around long enough to feel that there are times when the best thing to do is to power up the network, just to get things done. Turning to trusted, skilled members sometimes appears more reliable than running everything through a committee.

One challenge comes in judging when this casual, but effective approach benefits the congregation in the long run. This question probably will emerge, at least indirectly, during the evaluation of the lists. So make them as complete as you can before going on to the evaluation step.

### EVALUATE

At first, it may seem that little or nothing in your declaration of vision would bear much upon the "how" function. After all, the declaration speaks in grander terms, does it not? Well, not necessarily. Part of your vision could have to do with being deliberate about how people become active and how the organizational structure serves the congregation's ministry. Even if this were not explicitly included, however, the declaration's implications for "what" and "who" will affect "how." One reason for leaving this function for the last is that you already will have assessed and noted ideas for the other two functions. Some of the structural and procedural implications may have been touched on during the previous two discussion processes.

You can use three questions to focus your evaluation of "how." The first, and broadest, one is, *"How well do our present structures and processes help us accomplish our 'what' with the people we want to be involved?"* This question truly is evaluative, for it forces the issue of whether the horse is pulling the cart or not. You should be prepared for resistance here, for longtime members might feel as though the question is trying to "fix" something that "ain't broke." The hope is that the entire constellating process will have prepared all participants in this phase to see their congregation in new ways.

The second question is, *"Where can we trim down our structure to serve 'what' and 'who'?"* This question may be discussed more effectively in tandem with the third question, *"How can we learn to be flexible?"* Both questions seek to get at the matter of "how" serving the other three functions, not developing a life of its own.

In preparation for the action work on "how," the constellating team would benefit from a report by one of its members from the book *Sacred Cows Make Gourmet Burgers,* by William Easum.[3] Many ideas in this book will stir conversation. Most pertinent of these ideas to the "how" function is Easum's insistence that the hierarchical bureaucracies of the Industrial Age are now ill equipped to benefit organizational needs today.[4] Many denominations in the 1900s adopted this most common form of organizational structure. From 2000 and beyond, however, the organizations that will flourish will use more relational and flexible ways to operate. Some writers in business management call this new style "decentralization."[5]

For Easum, our familiar church organizational structures have become one of the church's most prevalent sacred cows. His ideas should help the group see some signs of "how" in its working declaration. See what your team and your "how" group do with these ideas as they answer the three questions above. Then you are ready to work on ideas for action.

### 5. "How": Suggest Action

For congregations that have been around for quite a few years, Easum advocates a specific direction for church organization. He promotes the concept of ministry teams, in which persons in the congregation with a driving concern for a particular need come together to serve that need.[6] These teams do not operate like committees, but they are enveloped within the congregation's vision, which provides all teams with their coherence and initial energy.

Some churches will conclude that Easum's ideas are too radical to use in any practical way. Other churches will see in *Sacred Cows Make Gourmet Burgers* a blueprint for reforming their "how" to serve their "why," their new declaration of vision. Easum knows, for instance, that our bureaucracies cannot be transformed overnight. Your "how" group might decide that a realistic approach would be to reduce your organizational structure by one-third in the next twelve months. Such a goal can be guided through effective decision making if the focus of the goal is kept on fulfilling your declaration of vision.

One congregation that had been losing members for years elected a young, newer member of the congregation as its new council chairperson. This energetic man could see that the monthly meeting schedule of all the church's committees—spread out across the calendar—made it difficult to share information and ideas effectively. It also drained the pastor's time and energy. He persuaded the church council to adopt a nine-month trial period, during which all committees would meet on the same night, ninety minutes before the regular council meeting. This arrangement would encourage committees to check with one another as they discussed plans and schedules. It would encourage them to do significant preliminary work between meetings, to better use their time. It also would let the pastor float between the committees and use other contacts during the month to help committee members prepare plans or actions.

Despite predictable objections, the council approved the plan. The following month, the trial schedule was inaugurated. Within six months, however, the old, familiar schedule was back in place. Hardly anyone besides the council chairperson noticed what had happened. This story illustrates how hard it is to change structure without a compelling motive larger than the decision itself.

A Mennonite congregation had struggled for two years with its finances and pastoral leadership before voting to dismiss its pastor. That decision decimated the mostly professional congregation; many members left and did not return. Those who remained felt the pain of the loss but still believed in the importance of their church's particular Anabaptist heritage of Christian witness. With such a loss of members, certain things had to be different. One of the first decisions was to simplify the number of official committees. The remaining members agreed to a reorganization into just three committees. "Us" would oversee worship, fellowship, and education; "Them" would work with mission activity and ecumenical ties; and "Stuff" would cover administrative and property matters. Although a couple of older members remained somewhat confused, the new structure served the recovering congregation well.

Whatever suggestions your group adopts, it is crucial that they can be linked to something that flows from the working declaration. Perhaps they relate directly to other suggestions prepared from your earlier discussions of "what" and "who." Perhaps they come from the group's recognition that some of the congregation's operational methods overlap each other or are redundant. Your team should recognize, even before the "how" is assessed, that a new vision cannot be implemented effectively without making at least some adjustments in the ways that the church does things.

## Transitions into Action

By the time that all three of the defining functions—"what," "who," and "how"—have been described and evaluated, and action has been suggested, your team will have launched the congregation into its new future. Perhaps it would be more accurate to qualify this statement with the phrase, "If you led each phase and step with care and preparation, then..."

One of the impressions that I hope to leave with you most strongly is that futuring your church does not happen automatically or easily. This process, which we have almost finished summarizing, is totally useless—and perhaps even harmful—if undertaken in a perfunctory manner. That is why, as I urged earlier, that a rhythm of spiritual disciplines should undergird and energize your futuring team all along the way. If you have not been sure of the prior leading of the Holy Spirit in your life or among the congregation's, you will come to trust in it here.

So let us presume that your team has been spiritually centered throughout this long, involved process. The team has engaged in each phase and set of activities with intelligence and prayer. The congregation and official board have stayed informed, interested, and trusting. The team has gathered all the notes from the activities outlined in this chapter. Now what?

At some point, the official leadership of your congregation needs to sign on to what the team has prepared the congregation to be and do. This might mean taking all the suggestions for action to a weekend retreat of the board and the team. It might mean taking one hour in each of three consecutive board meetings to discuss one of the three functions' findings. The particular format and timing depend upon your situation and your team's sense of what will be most effective. Know this, however: if the board rejects the suggestions categorically, the team failed months earlier. It failed to account for the particular cultural potency of the congregation and how that potency is not subject to reason alone. As your team has nurtured a spiritual centeredness to its own work, so also the board should have engaged in such practices during the futuring period. Sensitivity, trust, skilled conversation, openness, and creativity are all at stake here.

Your official board's actual vote on the working declaration of vision, on your fresh constellation to guide you into the future, should be taken once the team senses that it will be a symbolic moment. That is, the purpose of the vote is not in this case to argue the merits of the vision. Those arguments, if there are any, need to take place earlier, in each one of the phases of the process, expressed in a number of ways. Thus, the vote becomes the board's way of speaking for the congregation that "it has seemed good to the Holy Spirit and to us" (Acts 15:28) to follow the identified constellation.

How the board decides to treat the set of suggestions is again a matter of discretion based, in part, upon your congregation's polity. Implementing the action suggestions will take time; some could go into effect quickly, others will need a longer duration to accomplish. In all things, the main question now becomes, "Does this help us follow our fresh constellation?"

Because the future of your gospel witness is so important to God, seeing constructive results from all this work is absolutely essential. Let us turn to the last chapter to consider some hazards and hopes that await a church that is willing to embrace the future.

# Not Losing Heart

## The Perils and Promises of Futuring

# 7

M OST CHURCH PEOPLE recognize the burning bush as a symbol of high biblical drama. Moses, whose early life already had had more intrigue and glamour than most persons ever see in a lifetime, was living quietly as a nomadic shepherd. His new life with a wife and adopted clan was a far cry from his years in the Egyptian pharaoh's own household, as a grandson. Moses saw himself as different from the Midianites, for his cultural heritage was surely Egyptian (Exod. 2:16–20). Yet there he was, safely settled into a way of life common to the region and time.

What happened to Moses at the burning bush was totally unexpected. As the story implies, Moses was fairly satisfied with his new circumstances. Moses was not looking for any adventures. But Yahweh came to him anyway. It was time to do something about those ancestors of Abraham, Isaac, and Jacob, who were living under Pharaoh's thumb in Egypt. Yahweh, their God—yes, even Moses' God (Exod. 2:1–10)—was going to rescue them. And Moses was the one whom Yahweh had tapped to lead the people out. The palace-youth-turned-shepherd would have to convince the Israelites that he was representing their God. Then Moses and the elders would have to convince Pharaoh to let them go (Exod. 3:13–19). Pharaoh, the most powerful figure in their world, and Moses, his adopted grandson-turned-rebel. What a scenario!

In case you have never before noticed it in this story, Moses was not exactly enthusiastic about Yahweh's calling. First he questioned the appropriateness of his selection (Exod. 3:11). Then he asked for God's business card, to show to the others (Exod. 3:13). When those two tactics did not seem to deter God, Moses tried another angle: the Israelites would question his credibility as Yahweh's emissary. When Yahweh showed him a few tricks to use before the Egyptian magicians, Moses tried one last approach to dodge his selection for the task. He pleaded that he had no skill for speaking in public to inspire his people and impress the pharaoh. Alas, even that tactic backfired: God selected Aaron, Moses' brother, to do the talking, with Moses' prompting from Yahweh. His protests apparently exhausted, Moses then received permission from his father-in-law to undertake the journey back to Egypt. He was, as this summary plainly indicates, reluctant to have been given the responsibility. Yet it had come from God; he needed to follow it, even though it meant frustration and discouragement. What mattered in the long run was that God's promise, to the community that God had created, would be fulfilled.

### Courage to Follow God

The call of Moses symbolizes much of what today's congregations face as they consider their futures. Who among us is eager to leave what has been a comfortable life situation, to walk into new circumstances filled with unknown possibilities and dangers? Moses did not volunteer to lead his people. Yet the need for a new future was clear; Yahweh was ready to act on the Israelites' behalf; and the call to an unsuspecting shepherd was given. Despite his reluctance and protests, Moses took on the call— and the promise of God was accomplished. In the midst of all the details of the events in Exodus, the theme emerges that *God aims to bless those who, through trust, follow the calling into new territory.*

This theme of trust in following God more than merely recurs in the Bible: it rests at the heart of the biblical story. It faces characters, communities, and readers at almost every turn; it takes shapes that are sometimes hard to take; it forces people to make decisions that affect the course of their, and others', lives. Trust in following God has an edge of challenge to it, and sometimes that challenge does not appear savory.

Such certainly was the case with the so-called prophet Jonah. His calling was to take the message of God's expectations to the capital city of Israel's hated former conquerors (Jon. 1:1–2; 3:1–2). The most famous part of this story is Jonah's being swallowed by a whale ("large fish," 1:17);

when taken out of context, however, it misses the point entirely. Even the ocean depths cannot stop God from fulfilling a mission through one who is called. Jonah finally preached to his enemies, they changed their ways, and Jonah slunk off to sulk in anger (chaps. 3 and 4).

Those of you who have read all of this book might be feeling a bit like Moses and Jonah right now. Perhaps you, too, feel reluctantly called to help a community find its way with God. Perhaps that community reveals no concern as you understand the need. Perhaps the complainers and naysayers sound like the Israelites in the wilderness or Jonah heading for Tarshish.

In this chapter, we seek to treat some of the general issues that face a congregation willing to risk following God with a fresh constellation. Futuring your church should be an exhilarating and rewarding experience, but that does not mean that there are no deserts along the way. Having some idea what to anticipate can help your team with its skill level and its confidence.

Your church's fresh constellation—as expressed through the working declaration of vision—has been the goal to discern throughout most of the process outlined in this book. However, you realize by now that getting it on paper is not the end. A fresh constellation is to be discerned, yes, but it also needs to be articulated, promoted, shared, and followed. Chapter 6 was designed to get your team started on sharing and following. You can expect perils on that path, but also promises. In this chapter, let us look at some of the perils and promises. We will identify the perils in terms of strategy, power, vying "rationalities," theology, and the role of the pastor. For each category I offer some insights and suggestions for action. First, however, let us look at two sociological concepts that help to explain some of the most basic tension that futuring your church creates.

## A Phenomenon in Tension

For as long as we know, human beings have gathered in communities. In fact, at the level of procreation and child rearing, some level of human association seems always to have been necessary. Further, it appears that until recent centuries, most human association had been created without the feature of individual option. A person was born, raised, active, and finally disposed of in a network of social relationships and expectations that were given, not negotiated.

The religious landscape in the United States functions for the most part in a distinctly different context from this ancient one. Today, continuing a trend that has been in evidence at least since the Great Awakening, religious affiliation is affected more and more by individual choice than by group inheritance. One of the effects of choice in religion is especially evident when we observe the life history of any particular church tradition. This effect can be illuminated usefully with the tandem sociological concepts of movement and institution.[1]

These two concepts describe the two poles of a spectrum that constitutes group behavior. When human beings get together to pursue certain purposes and activities, they do so initially with a predictable set of characteristics. These include focus upon a newly defined mission, enthusiasm, adaptability, task sharing, high commitment, brief life span, threat of instability and rapid dissolution, charismatic leadership, and the like. A group venture expressing such characteristics is a *movement,* for it is still in flux and vulnerable to many factors. A movement that survives eventually takes on a life of its own. When this happens, the concern for continuity becomes replaced by steadiness in activity, participation levels, structures, and energy. Maintaining what has worked in the past is a high value in this kind of social group, the *institution.* Empires, traditional bureaucracies, corporations, government divisions, and other modern social groups are all subject to this process.

So are congregations. If we used these two concepts of movement and institution to describe the goal of futuring your church, we would say that its purpose is to find creative ways to balance both movement-like and institutional features. Enthusiasm, clear focus, high commitment (movement)—all must work together with sustainable features (institution). Realistically, though, most congregations with a substantial history need more movementlike than institutional qualities. Church renewal and vitality today must recapture the spirit and feel of new movements.[2]

The practical implications of this sociological analysis of congregations should be fairly clear. Your team—and gradually your ruling church board—should become adept at seeking in your congregation a creative tension. It is a tension because, if it goes away, an established church will begin to ossify. It is creative because finding constructive solutions to the pull between the two forces is the only way to keep the church strong in the long run. That is, the bad news is that a congregation with a fresh constellation will have to deal with tension between familiar things that are comfortable and new things that are possible. The good news is that this tension is the intersection for your congregation's meaningful ministry in the future.

## Perils to the Church with a Fresh Constellation

With this sociological framework, let us elaborate on the several perils mentioned earlier, as they could affect your team's ability to continue the futuring process.

### Strategy

Being deliberate about the team's strategy is a constant priority. Here are three ways that neglect could cause your futuring to backfire.

INSIGHTS

Congregations that discover and renew themselves with fresh vision do not stumble along blindly. They need leaders who will persist with the process. The danger to the congregation is that those who commit to the church's future will abandon the venture before it is well under way. This may occur for a number of reasons. One is getting sidetracked by issues that appear to be necessary but will drain away time and energy from the original task. If you remember the four functions—"why," "what," "who," and "how"—it will be easier for you to spot a rabbit trail. Another reason for abandonment is an unexpected crisis, such as a natural disaster or other community or congregational tragedy. However, the leaders—your team—would be prepared to help the board and church interpret the incident in terms of your long-range purpose.

One church began a visioning process in which many church leaders participated and which was well received. After a few meetings, however, the pastor seemed to have lost sight of the purpose. He offered good-sounding reasons for delaying the next steps. He privately criticized the church for being apathetic. By the time an assessment phase was held, the planning group had dwindled, the pastor's contributions to the phase confused the issues, and the lay leaders began to scatter on summer vacations. The process was not allowed to run its course. This church had inadvertently aborted the fresh vision. The leaders had not understood that there are times when following a process is what a church needs; sometimes our life together depends upon agreeing to a discipline and staying with it to its fullness.

Another strategic peril rests in the team's interpretation of the process to the congregation. Earlier chapters include an emphasis in each phase upon the team engaging the congregation. This involves more than mere reporting. Certainly, the congregation needs to know what the team is up to. The congregation also needs to know why the team—with the official board's approval—has engaged in this process. If the purpose, outline, and excitement of the team are not effectively conveyed, seeds of failure could be sown, seeds that might sprout into thorns instead of the desired crop. Take your communication and interpretation roles seriously as well as creatively.

Finally, your futuring strategy can become imperiled by its pacing. Some congregations have participated in mission statement processes that were collapsed into one weekend or three meetings held over three or four months. As I indicated earlier, a truly transformative futuring experience takes some time. The greater tendency and temptation are to suppose that a truly dynamic constellation can emerge for your church with only a minimum effort of energy and time.

If, however, we recognize that fresh constellations call forth a fresh spin on your congregation's culture, time and patience are essential. No cultural change can occur quickly. The more your fresh constellation moves away from things as they are, the more change will be necessary to the culture. Futuring your church is not like the popular and glib "been there, done that" cliché. Pacing can make a big difference.

SUGGESTIONS

With these three insights in mind, here are three practical ideas that can help your team. First, and perhaps foremost, secure the earnest and willing commitment of the pastor and key congregational leaders. They should believe that this constellating experience is the top priority for the church during this time. How this network of key persons reaches this point of common commitment will vary, depending upon who initially promotes the idea. The pastor and church leaders need one another if the enterprise is to succeed.

Second, turn the church's calendar of events for the coming year into opportunities to interpret and promote the process. Create ways to relate each phase of the constellation, as well as the resulting working declaration, to congregational groups and programs. Do not underestimate the importance of these opportunities. Part of the creativity will come in the ways that the project is shared. Members who are apathetic or feel threatened will not respond well to a repetitious, predictable format. Your team is leading the way into your congregation's new future. The congregation must become convinced, even before you share the working declaration for the first time, that this activity is of primary importance.

One approach to this interpretive challenge would be to enlist one or two of the congregation's most creative members to act as the team's promotion think tank. They could receive regular summaries of the process and work on ideas that fit well with your progress at any given point. Early on, the team as a whole could look at the calendar to pinpoint significant places and events. Do not allow your work with the team to drift away from the lifeblood of the congregation.

Third, enlist the congregation's official ruling body as a major player in the constellation experience. Develop a way for the members of that formal group to be eyes and ears into the congregation. Set aside regular docket time for sharing what these board members are hearing and observing that pertain to the futuring process. "How is it going? What are people saying? Where is the team going at this point?" These questions should be engaged in a probing but constructive way. It will help this body to perform this task effectively if it also adopts a spiritual discipline during the process. Shaping the board's business in an atmosphere of devotion will invigorate and augment the constellation experience. A book such as Olsen's *Transforming Church Boards into Communities of Spiritual Leaders* provides useful guidance for such a venture.[3]

## Power
Church leaders often seem reluctant to address issues of power. Your team cannot afford to be timid here. Let us look at a couple of definitions that can help your team avoid being caught off-guard.

INSIGHTS

Simply stated, power is the ability to make things happen. Most well-established congregations have members whose power is substantial, even if their official authority—vested through appointment or vote—is not, at a given time, significant. Sometimes in a congregation's life, a member or two disagree with a particular decision or action and decide that they have enough power to resist or undo the action. If their resistance or "undoing" flows through recognized and accepted congregational channels, their use of power probably is appropriate. However, church members do not always "play fair." It is amazing in certain situations to observe what members (or pastors and staff, for that matter) might do to get their way. Your team possibly could run into a similar situation or two during the constellation experience.

Power is a complex phenomenon that at times can seem elusive to understand. Yet in the cultural model that we are utilizing in this book, power can be illuminated and anticipated in some very helpful ways. We begin to realize, for instance, that power is vested within the culture rather than simply being the province of individual persons. In a very real way, then, the church member who seeks to force his or her way can do so only if the church's culture permits it.

Another related concept can further elucidate the relationship of power and culture. It is the concept of subculture. As we saw in chapter 6, "subculture" can be defined as *a variation within the general culture under consideration, in which certain features are shared with the larger culture and others are distinct from it.* This definition means that what qualifies as a subculture depends upon its context, its environment. Lutheran Germans in Germany might be part of the German macroculture, but in the United States they form a mesoculture (i.e., a subculture). Chinatowns create their own subcultures within their foreign cities' microcultures. Even with the limits of an organization, subcultures can and do exist, depending in part upon their size, the complexity of their environment, the nature of their mission, and so on.

Your congregation probably has subcultures. They often tend to be defined by groups with their own particular histories within that of the church, but the subculture is felt beyond the group itself. In many long-established congregations, a subculture is often most evident in the choir, a couples' club, or a women's association. These organizations within the church tend to draw persons to participate over periods of time. Peculiarities of activity and habit develop. Relationships with other groups become defined in certain ways. Individuals from these groups take on roles of varying responsibility within the church. As the years go by, perspectives, attitudes, and implicit understandings emerge among and between these groups. Sometimes the subculture reveals agendas that indirectly suggest greater loyalty than to those of the congregation as a whole.

If there is any validity to scrutinizing congregational realities with an anthropological lens, then it becomes apparent that subcultures create forms of power. The ability of one person to persuade others to adopt an idea or plan depends upon the operating culture's resonance with the point for persuasion. That is, there is an important sense in which an individual never acts alone: she or he inhabits a particular world in which certain behaviors are more likely and others less so. The ability of a person to "make things happen"—that is, power—is linked to the dynamics of the immediate culture in which the person is acting. Both the temper of that culture and its current state of strength will influence the way in which power will be exercised. In turn, the subcultures within that culture develop their roles and potential for power based upon that wider culture.

This explanation might appear to be complicated, and one point to make here is that it indeed can be so. The action of power within a congregation can (unfortunately) become as convoluted and intriguing as any corporate scandal. Those of us in congregations would do well to avoid simplistic interpretations of contests over power, even when the sequence of action and the players seem straightforward. I suggest instead to look for the signs of the congregation's various subcultures at stake in the contest.

Matters where power is very much at stake often appear in the congregation's public arena only when pastoral or staff performance comes into question. One all too common version of this performance issue arises when a slowly declining, older congregation, in an oblique attempt to shore up its membership and programming, hires an energetic pastor to "help bring in more young people." Subcultures in congregations often run along generational lines. The retirement-age members want the church to survive their lifetimes, but they do not quite bank on the differing interests and styles that young families seek out in a congregation. Their gung ho new pastor distributes flyers in the new subdivisions on the edge of town, makes a couple of changes in worship, uses contemporary idioms and illustrations in her sermons, talks the music committee into buying a songbook to complement the very traditional hymnal, organizes field trips for older children, and takes twenty children of brand-new families to church camp the next summer.

At the end of her first year, the pastor begins to hear veiled comments from older church members during her regular calls to their homes. She assures them that the church is growing as the search committee had wanted. Two months later, a contingent of longtime, older members appear at the monthly board meeting, with a petition requesting a return to specific worship practices and discontinuation of virtually all the new programs initiated by the pastor. Pandemonium prevails during that meeting. Board members, mostly middle-aged and younger, are caught off guard, although most of them had heard rumors about complaints.

When contests in the church surface, and power is at stake, what steps can be taken to handle the matter with the least damage? And what notions about the nature of such incidents will provide the most useful interpretation of what is taking place?

SUGGESTIONS

Not all power in congregations is evident only during disagreements, but disagreements certainly underscore the existence of congregational power. Stated another way, one of the goals for a church with a fresh constellation is to intentionally negotiate the use of power. Some of the negotiations must be undertaken as your church's "how" function is assessed. More generally, however, you will do well to include in your working declaration some statement about the ways in which church members are encouraged to participate in the fellowship. This statement will reflect both theological conviction and practical implications for the use of power.

The concept of subcultures enhances your ability to analyze upcoming decisions for any possible points of contest. If power is understood as a means of putting your working declaration into action, the notion of subcultures helps your team sort out the scenarios without having to fall into a "win-lose" stance.

What is a common scenario for the board meeting mentioned above? Often a line is drawn in the sand; the protesters claim that something is wrong and should be righted; supporters of the new practices defend them; eventually, someone questions the pastor's suitability. Tempers rise; patience runs in short supply; and the church is on the brink of losing momentum.

Using the concept of subculture, then, we can identify one major way that congregational power can be approached. All issues in the congregation's futuring process can be framed in terms of the existing dominant subculture responding to a new culture that is seeking to emerge. This new, as yet nascent, culture is perceived by those who share most strongly in the dominant subculture as something that contends for the loyalty of church members.

That is, if the new culture gets a following, the dominant one will play a different role in the church, if not seriously fade. This perception—a fairly accurate one—creates a concern for control, stability, the congregation's ability to do things—power. The extent of a struggle between the two subcultures depends upon the degree of change that the working declaration of vision represents.

Again, the value of seeing church power in terms of subcultures is that it offers a wider and less defensive interpretation of what is at stake in church decisions. Pitting the preferences of individuals or groups against one another usually degenerates into finger-pointing and questioning another person's judgment or motives. When church members can reframe the same potentially stressful situations as the result of different subcultures in the same congregation, they can focus more effectively upon the bigger picture: "What should our future become?"

This view of power also helps us see why your team and ruling board should not acquiesce to demands from members who are not cooperating with the futuring process. This is not to say that your team or ruling board should treat protests and concerns with a callous air. If, however, you have engaged each phase of this process as outlined in this book, giving care to informing and involving church members and groups along the way, you will have had plenty of opportunities to find out where the "rubs" might be located. Anticipating issues and resistance by persons and groups will serve the process better than fighting fires. Ways to prepare for constructive communication have been discussed in each chapter.

## Vying "Rationalities"

INSIGHTS

There is an aspect of culture that expands upon culture's relationship with power. It should be fairly evident by now that cultures develop their own ways of how things make sense. We can use the term "rationality" to describe the sense-making function that culture plays. What is normal practice in one culture can appear quite odd, or even disturbing, in another culture. In both cultures, however, what is done is considered reasonable, rational. One example is occupations. In the United States, most persons are free to pursue their own interests and develop the skill and experience necessary for this or that career. By contrast, cultures in a number of other parts of the world view this freedom of occupation with disbelief. Such a decision is made instead on the basis of gender, birth order, family position, and wealth—by the person's parents, and sometimes only the men (i.e., father, grandfather, uncle). The two paths to occupation are quite different, yet both make sense within their respective cultures.

Second, related to this sense-making function is the manner in which stagnant congregations use their rationality. The culture of a well-established congregation that is steadily losing members turns backward-looking. It views its present and future increasingly in terms of its past, even as the present becomes less and less like that past. This results in a sense-making style that becomes "irrational," that is, is less and less capable of understanding the congregation's existence in light of current circumstances. Irrationality becomes rationalization for continuing practices (what) and processes (how) that contribute to the church's decline rather than its vitality.

A third insight about rationality reveals more about where your church's fresh constellation will meet resistance. Persons who deeply represent the congregation's dominant subculture can feel that anything new is a threat. Such persons tend to focus upon issues without ever identifying them as potential symbols of a budding subculture. Two ways that this indirect resistance often appears are by protesting against changes in a long-established, cherished activity or by questioning the pastor's competence or fit with the congregation. It is easier to point fingers at something concrete ("Our pastor does not call on homebound persons enough") than it is to recognize what is at stake in the bigger picture of the congregation's future.

I was working with a dwindling congregation whose almost sole constituency gradually had moved miles away. The church board agreed to do some visioning work, to look at their heritage, their neighborhood, and their bearings. One board member was especially enthusiastic to begin. He encouraged others to take part. We were about halfway through the process when I called him to check on some information. His manner over the phone was distant, quite different from before. It did not take him long to explain the change of tone. "How could you [do such-and-such, part of the training process]? How could you ask [so-and-so] to do [such-and-such]? You are wasting our time and money, and I have told the others so." This lifelong member of the congregation was so caught up in the congregation's irrational culture that he could not grant credence to the process that I was following. As he saw it, the problem was with what I was doing, not with the congregation's deep stagnation. Needless to say, the congregation did not discover a fresh constellation for itself. We finished the process as best we could, but this one member had "poisoned the well." The irrationality of the congregation's culture was so strong that it threw off attempts to help it understand things differently.

SUGGESTIONS

The first suggestion for dealing with cultural irrationality has been discussed several times already. Your team should be intentional about how it helps the futuring process make sense in your congregation. Being very deliberate and specific about connecting with your church's folkways will pay off later.

Second, the team should discuss and agree together what team members will say to respond to the comment, "Everything is fine. Why do we need to change anything?" The response by team members is a key point at which the constellating process can be interpreted and encouraged. If you allow, by neglect, team members to say whatever they think of saying, you are weakening the congregation's chance to begin learning a new rationality.

For instance, it probably would be best to answer the "Why do we have to do this?" question with another question. You want the questioner to make the same kind of internal connection between the intentionality and a healthy future that the team has made. Asking, "Where will this congregation be fifteen years from now?" propels the issue toward its appropriate direction. "Doing exactly what it is doing now" might be the questioner's answer. It is possible to respond to such an optimistic response by saying, "Yes, our congregation might look much the same in fifteen years. The futuring process prepares us to stay strong and faithful, even if things begin to change. We would rather be in a position to decide our own direction than to have something unpleasant forced on us." Such an answer helps to focus on a desired situation for any church culture: to be able to determine its own life rather than be limited by unanticipated circumstances. Again, remember that the purpose of being prepared with such an answer is not to win an argument, but to clarify and frame the futuring experience in a positive way.

Third, keep the process and any discussions about it within the congregation's public arena. Head off any signs that members or organizations may be confused, distressed, or contemplating resistance. This suggestion does not contradict the one above, about not giving in to naysayers. Here, you are being proactive all along the way. The question constantly in front of your team is, "Do they understand what is happening and what it is for?" When team members encounter a need to interpret, they should have practiced ahead of time asking questions rather than simply making statements. Asking questions such as, "What do you think the team is trying to do for the church?"; "What do you think are the big issues that our church has to deal with in the next ten years?"; and "What will make this church thrive twenty-five years from now?" can give team members a chance to find out more about the recalcitrant member's views; he or she might not have had a chance yet to air them or even to think about them. Asking such questions also impels the recalcitrant member to articulate a future. Too often, longtime members are so committed to a waning subculture that the future is hard to consider on its own terms. Use these encounters to draw out a genuine dialogue, one that will further—not scuttle—the futuring process.

## Theology

INSIGHTS

A silent tragedy that points to a need for renewal is the loss in many churches of theological thinking. As I noted in chapter 1, the religious landscape in the United States has been changing significantly since the 1960s. It should generate concern to realize that the numerical and civic decline of mainline Protestantism has been accompanied by a widespread inability to speak of, and reflect upon, faith. Too many churches function with theological understanding that has not developed past a sixth-grade church school level. It reminds me of a middle-aged man in one of the congregations that I served some years ago. He hardly ever came to church for anything, although he said that, when he did, he wanted sermons to give him moral guidance. I would hope that sermons would help people decide how to behave as Christians. Yet this particular church member wanted the morality without the theology. Churches that do not link the two closely together are eventually doomed.

There is a fear among some members of churches that serious engagement in theology requires rigid thinking, dogmatic positions that are not "modern," "intelligent," or practical. Such concern is founded on a narrow view of the theological task—as though the only "real" theology is so convinced of its own truth that questioners need not apply. Theology is not limited to dogmatic assertions on either end of the spectrum. Similarly, some church members assume that the only authentic theology is what seminary professors, who are specially educated, get paid to do. I hope that you do not believe this. Instead, I earnestly intend that you take the challenge that John Cobb presents to today's once mainline churches. Cobb, a retired professional theologian and one of my teachers, argues that lay people in churches need to learn to think about their faith and its view of life. In fact, Cobb claims that theological thinking by church people is necessary if our churches are to embrace new vitality.[4]

This process of futuring offers your congregation the opportunity to begin a crisp emphasis upon theological thinking. Likely, it will need to take a recognizable form, such as retreats, classes, or study groups. I was dumbfounded once when an active churchwoman told me that I was the first pastor since she had joined that congregation to teach a class for adults. She had been a member there forty years. Perhaps one of the corollaries to the mainline malaise has been the low commitment by many pastors to the ministry of teaching.

## SUGGESTIONS

Many readers belong to a denominational tradition that publishes educational materials. When was the last time that someone in your congregation—other than the pastor or Christian education director—looked at a catalog of your denominational resources? Curriculum editors have worked hard over the years to provide a broad variety of educational materials that can be used in the congregation. There are Bible study series for various levels of preparation, guides for faith and life, guides for engaging public issues, historical surveys of your tradition and its theological idiosyncrasies, and so forth. These resources can stimulate a group of adults to venture with some confidence into an arena in which many have not trod.

More particularly, a study of your particular tradition can function as a springboard for theological development. What does it mean to be a Methodist, Disciple, Episcopalian today? How does your tradition frame its view of God, the Bible, salvation, and life in the world in ways that can translate into informed living now? Your congregation might discover this approach to be the most stimulating, especially if it is presented in an inviting manner.

The one place in the congregation's life that members usually have the most consistent opportunity to be exposed to theological thinking is the sermon. There has been a tendency in many churches during my lifetime for sermons to focus upon resources for daily living at the expense of clarifying their theological foundations. If John Cobb is right, then the sermon should become one place where theological reflection—and affirmation—occurs. Of course, to maintain its emphasis upon proclamation, preaching needs to function differently from a lecture. A sermon is never authentically about reasonableness alone. Its purpose is to lift up some aspect of the gospel witness as it lays claim upon the lives of listeners. Yet toward this purpose, skilled preaching can provoke theological development as well as instill hope, conviction, and guidance.

These comments point eventually to the work of the pastor. One central pastoral role that needs recovering is that of congregational theologian. The one with (usually) the most extensive formal training in theology should be alert to creative ways of spurring theological activity in the congregation. For many churches, this particular pastoral challenge will seem new. Its place in future congregational vitality, however, is central.

As we conclude our look at some of the hazards to futuring your church, the pastoral role itself deserves a bit more attention.

## The Pastoral Role

INSIGHTS

Your church's pastor faces a paradox. Genuine congregational health and fresh direction *cannot happen* without her or him, but at the same time, it cannot *be about* him or her. The role of the pastor, especially when a church seeks new life, must concentrate upon what is good for the congregation rather than upon what is of particular interest to the pastor. When a church depends primarily upon its pastor for its sense of well-being and security, strong congregational identity and mission will not be possible. A dynamic church emerges when the pastor is able to help it see a picture in the sky of God's call to it, and then to inspire the people to pursue that picture with energy, intelligence, imagination, and love. If the pastor puts more energy into following his or her special career concerns than into the congregation's authentic gospel well-being, eventually the congregation will suffer.

Earlier, we noted that two ways that a pastor can make distinctive contributions to fresh vitality are through attention to preaching and teaching. One implication of this emphasis is worthy of note, for it changes the way that churches think about—and search for—a pastor. The pastor's role in vital futuring calls for a shift away from so much weight upon administration and pastoral care.

To explain more of what this claim means, consider the organizational diamond, which was introduced in the previous chapter, to use in applying new vision to congregational life. Administration tends to focus upon operations and management, which centers in the "how" function. Pastoral care concentrates upon the well-being of church members and families, those who constitute some (but, remember, not all) of the congregation's "who." By contrast, teaching and preaching are activities (what) that stimulate the church's awareness of and commitment to its vision (why). The point is not that administration and pastoral care are useless congregational concerns—not at all. Both sets of ministry tasks can be performed with clear attention to their contributions to church vitality. However, many churches in the last couple of generations have put a low premium upon the pastor's role as a teacher. Similarly, many look for sermons not to challenge them theologically, just to placate them psychologically or spiritually.

That is, a church that wants a pastor primarily to keep things running smoothly and to help the church members feel good is a church without a future.

SUGGESTIONS

The following comments, then, are directed toward pastors who are motivated to shape their ministry to benefit their congregations first of all. For one thing, you might have to learn to talk to yourself differently. Thoughts such as, *This is not about me, but about the future of this church's vital Christian witness,* can help to put your work in perspective. They help you distinguish between who you are as a person and what the church needs (not wants) from the pastoral role right now. Second, view your pastoral work within the framework of leadership for vision. This is a broader perspective than often is followed. Focus upon the congregation as a community and upon the gifts that members can exercise in service of a desired future. Third, take initiative to establish yourself as the congregation's theologian-in-residence.

You as pastor have been prepared for this capacity by your preparation for ordination. The futuring process grants you a reason and permission to lead the congregation's theological maturation. Of course, depending upon the congregation's current health and interest, you will need to approach this task with care. You will want to ascertain its cultural comfort as you formulate creative ways to engage members and groups.

## The Promises of Futuring Your Church

In an age that seeks one quick, unconnected experience after another, you and your team can live for promises that persist. One promise is that you have learned to do something that will be valuable again and again. The futuring process is a reflective pattern that your church's leadership can utilize as part of its ongoing rhythm. Once you have walked through the process a first time, it will be easier to do again in a few years. Most of the gathered material will remain pertinent; you will look a second time mostly for the new developments and their importance. Ironically, it is also easier to maintain and adapt vision when it is clear and still fairly strong. Depending upon environmental changes of any kind, your new constellation could serve you, with minor modifications, for years to come. This book shows you how to get this pattern and rhythm started in your church.

Second, you have the promise of showing your congregation how rich the ancient metaphor of the body of Christ can be today. If anything results from the team's efforts, it should be a heightened sense of the congregation as community. The purpose of the church is to become not a filling station for individuals but a commonwealth of believers drawn together in shared ministry and mission. Along the way, your team will experience tastes of this commonwealth and will be prepared to diffuse its energy among the congregation.

Third, you hold the promise of empowering your church. Your work is not aimed at allowing a select few to be privy to the "secrets" of your activity. Rather, by engaging more and more church members in various stages, the team can stimulate their own gifts and abilities. As members talk, listen, and reflect, interests and skills that perhaps have sat dormant could be sparked. You want this momentum to be created.

Fourth, empowerment means that the team can model a different way of exercising power. In truth, the congregation's culture bears the power, dispensing it—so to speak—through the highways and byways of its multifaceted expression. Congregations with a fresh, embraced constellation are eager to allow persons to do what they can to be part of the vision. It reminds me of what one consultant experienced in his first staff meeting with a church. When he entered the room, he was introduced to nine people, by first and last names only, all of whom were members of the church staff. The meeting proceeded for an hour with energetic participation by all. Finally, the consultant politely interrupted the group to ask which person had which position. After an hour, the consultant had not been able to distinguish the senior pastor from the secretary, the music director from the youth minister. What a testimony to sharing power.

Fifth, the team holds the promise of helping give birth to a new congregational culture. How different or similar this new culture will be, compared to the present one, is a question that will vary among congregations. In most cases, however, the team should be aware at the outset of its work that when it is all over, some things are going to be different. And I do not mean simply having a document that the board and congregation approved. Change in the congregation's culture is probably the biggest challenge in this entire experience. It is, however, also the most rewarding. The future will be different; it does not have to be completely unfamiliar or scary; it offers a new heaven and a new earth (Rev. 21:1) that will shape your church's way of being and doing.

Last, you hold the promise of a congregation becoming confident as theological actors. You will know that the new constellation is shaping a new culture when you hear church members saying, "We do this because of what we understand God to be like." Your congregation will not be embarrassed or reticent about talking theologically. Even more important, members will begin to make decisions at home and for parish ministry on the basis of their energized convictions. Such confidence will be one key fruit of your team's work, a symbolic affirmation that your congregation indeed has found its future.

As your church enters the future, may it know the love, patience, courage, and wisdom that only God provides.

# NOTES

## 1. Calling—Being Intentional about Your Church's Future

1. C. Kirk Hadaway and David A. Roozen, *Rerouting the Protestant Mainstream: Sources of Growth and Opportunities for Change* (Nashville: Abingdon Press, 1995), 24.

2. See Wade Clark Roof and William McKinney, *American Mainline Religion: Its Changing Shape and Future* (New Brunswick, N.J.: Rutgers University Press, 1987), 73–76.

3. Ibid., 73, 105.

4. Hadaway and Roozen, *Rerouting the Protestant Mainstream*, 40–53.

5. Ibid., 75–76.

6. Roof and McKinney, *American Mainline Religion*, 250.

7. As suggested by Hadaway and Roozen: "The vast majority of unchurched Americans has slight interest in conservative Christian programming or in restricting their lifestyle choices" (*Rerouting the Protestant Mainstream*, 53).

8. Ibid., 62.

9. Ibid., 68.

10. Ibid., 65.

11. Ibid., 87.

12. See ibid., 114–16, for their comments about denominational structures becoming more movementlike.

13. Lovett H. Weems Jr., *Church Leadership: Vision, Team, Culture, and Integrity* (Nashville: Abingdon Press, 1993), 40–45.

14. Ibid., 62–66.

15. Jeffrey Abrahams, *The Mission Statement Book* (Berkeley, Calif.: Ten Speed Press, 1995).

16. Ibid., 40.

17. Weems, *Church Leadership*, 40–41.

18. For more about teamwork in church leadership, see Weems, *Church Leadership,* chap. 3.

### 2. Heritage—Where Your Church Has Been and What It Means

1. A basic summary of cultural elements, and their application to modern organizations, is available in Andrew M. Pettigrew, "On Studying Organizational Cultures," *Administrative Science Quarterly* 24, no. 4 (1979): 570–81. A more accessible version, comprehensively developed and applied to modern organizations, is available in Edgar H. Schein, *Organizational Culture and Leadership,* 2d ed. (San Francisco: Jossey-Bass, 1992).

2. See Terrence E. Deal and Allen A. Kennedy, *Corporate Cultures: The Rites and Rituals of Corporate Life* (Reading, Mass.: Addison-Wesley, 1982), chap. 1.

### 4. Theological Bearings—What It Means for You to Be God's People

1. Benton Johnson, Dean R. Hoge, and Donald A. Luidens, "Mainline Churches: The Real Reason for Decline," *First Things,* March 1993, 13–18.

2. Ana Gobledale, *The Learning Spirit: Lessons from South Africa* (St. Louis: Chalice Press, 1995).

3. Tom Montgomery-Fate, *Beyond the White Noise: Mission in a Multicultural World* (St. Louis: Chalice Press, 1997).

4. Charles Bayer, *Hope for the Mainline Church* (St. Louis: CBP Press, 1991).

5. John M. Buchanan, *Being Church, Becoming Community* (Louisville: Westminster John Knox Press, 1996).

6. Donald W. Musser and Joseph L. Price, eds., *A New Handbook of Christian Theology* (Nashville: Abingdon Press, 1992).

7. John B. Cobb Jr., *Becoming a Thinking Christian* (Nashville: Abingdon Press, 1993).

8. Ibid., 7.

9. One possible resource for beginning theology is my *Foundations: Basics of the Christian Faith for Youth* (Nashville: Graded Press, 1988), 2 vols. Although *Foundations* is written for youth and young adults, the leader's guides make useful resources for an adult course.

10. See Eugene TeSelle, "Atonement," in *A New Handbook of Christian Theology*, 41–43, for an outline of this subject.

## 5. Futuring—Finding Your Church's Vision

1. For a concise but helpful delineation of the meaning of value-rationality, in contrast with other forms of social action and authority, see Joyce Rothschild-Whitt, "The Collectivist Organization: An Alternative to Rational-Bureaucratic Models," *American Sociological Review* 44 (August 1979): 509–10.

2. See James Luther Adams, *Voluntary Associations: Socio-Cultural Analyses and Theological Interpretation* (Chicago: Exploration Press, 1986), 250–53.

3. Alfred North Whitehead, *Process and Reality*, corrected edition, ed. David Ray Griffin and Donald W. Sherburne (New York: Free Press, 1978), 259.

4. Roy M. Oswald and Robert E. Friedrich Jr., *Discerning Your Congregation's Future: A Strategic and Spiritual Approach* (Bethesda, Md.: Alban Institute, 1996); see "Introduction: Discernment, Theology, and Prayer," Appendix A: "Guidelines for Fasting," and Appendix C: "Centering Prayer."

5. One resource for guided imagery meditations is Carolyn Stahl Bohler, *Opening to God* (Nashville: Upper Room, 1977).

6. Michael Slaughter, *Spiritual Entrepreneurs: Six Principles for Risking Renewal* (Nashville: Abingdon Press, 1995), 134–35.

## 6. Moving Ahead—Making Your Vision Work

1. For more on the four organizational functions, see Ichak Adizes, *Corporate Lifecycles: How Corporations Grow and Die and What You Can Do about It* (Englewood Cliffs, N.J.: Prentice-Hall, 1988), chap. 5.

2. Two recent books are among many newer titles aimed at helping older mainstream Protestant congregations rediscover spiritual vitality. *Practicing Our Faith: A Way of Life for a Searching People*, ed. Dorothy C. Bass (San Francisco: Jossey-Bass, 1997), provides chapters covering a number of practices with biblical and traditional roots; the book can be studied by individuals and by groups. John Ackerman, *Spiritual Awakening: A Guide to Spiritual Life in Congregations* (Baltimore: Alban Institute, 1994), uses several recent theories and models to frame a program

of practical spiritual growth that moves from individuals to the congregation. A growing interest in spirituality is providing motivated lay readers with a choice of helpful guides.

3. Willam M. Easum, *Sacred Cows Make Gourmet Burgers: Ministry Anytime, Anywhere, by Anyone* (Nashville: Abingdon Press, 1995).

4. Ibid., 97–101.

5. See Adizes, *Corporate Lifecycles,* 30–41.

6. Easum, *Sacred Cows Make Gourmet Burgers,* chap. 9.

## 7. Not Losing Heart—the Perils and Promises of Futuring

1. For a summary of the concepts of movement and institution, see R. Stephen Warner, *New Wine in Old Wineskins: Evangelicals and Liberals in a Small-Town Church* (Berkeley: University of California Press, 1988), 45–47.

2. For a discussion of denominational renewal in light of these two concepts, see Hadaway and Roozen, *Rerouting the Protestant Main-stream,* chap. 6.

3. Charles Olsen, *Transforming Church Boards into Communities of Spiritual Leaders* (Baltimore: Alban Institute, 1995).

4. Cobb, *Becoming a Thinking Christian,* 7–10.